CLIMBING
BIG WALLS

<u>Contributors to the book include:</u>
Jim Bridwell
Steve Grossman
Randy Leavitt
John Middendorf
Steve Schnieder
Mike Strassman

Edited by Mike Strassman

CLIMBING BIG WALLS

Illustrations by John McMullen

ICS BOOKS, INC.
Merrillville, Indiana

CLIMBING BIG WALLS

PUBLISHER'S NOTE

Acknowledgements

Many thanks to Neil Strassman who tediously edited this book and made suggestions; Steve Grossman, who double-checked explanations and descriptons to assure accuracy; and Eden Masters, who urged me to finish it so that I could climb more Big Walls.

Library of Congress Cataloging-in-Publication Data

Strassman, Michael A.
    Climbing big walls : intensive instruction for ascending vertical walls / by Michael Strassman.
        p.   cm.
    ISBN 0-934802-59-9 : $8.95
    1. Rock climbing.   I. Title.
GV200.2.S79 1990
796.5 ' 223--dc20   90-34049
                                                     CIP

TABLE OF CONTENTS

INTRODUCTION

By Michael A. Strassman

There is only one pre-requisite for climbing big walls— Experience!

In big wall climbing, there is no such thing as natural ability, as there is in sport climbing. Big wall climbing is far more technical and requires thorough organization, adept skill and good judgement. These come with experience.

How does one gain experience, without climbing big walls? You begin slowly, by working up to it. Climb longer routes, famililiarize yourself with setting up belays, hauling loads and living on the wall. Also, seek the advice of those who are more knowledgable about big walls. That is what this book is about, gaining experience.

Assembled in this book are tips and techniques by the finest big wall climbers of today. They will give you the instruction and advice necessary to climb any of the popular routes on El Capitan in Yosemite Valley. This book assumes that you have a working knowledge of belay and anchor systems and have substantial leading experience. A thorough understanding of placing protection, nut craft, and rope dynamics is also required. If you don't understand any of these techniques, find a certified mountain guide. He will give you some experience.

Likewise, don't jump on El Capitan for your first big wall. Try the Washington Column, then Half Dome. Once you feel secure in your technique, tackle the Big Stone. It will be one of the most memorable experiences of your life.

A big wall is any climb that takes about a full day or more, climbing at a moderate pace. Living on the wall becomes an intrinsic part of the experience. This is where the thrill comes in. You live and move through the vertical world, absorbing each undulation of rock, aware of every suspended moment.

John Middendorf, has quietly ascended El Capitan over 20 times. Known among Valley locals as "The Duece", John brings us the basic instruction for climbing a big wall. He believes in taking much of the mystery out of big wall climbing and in conveying his craft to all climbers. His equipment company, A5 Adventures, specializes in big wall outfitting and has helped many beginning wall climbers reach new heights.

Randy Leavitt has produced some of the toughest pitches ever climbed on El Cap. The hardest aid climbing designation, A5, is synomonous with Mr. Leavitt's bold climbing style. However, Randy is a very safe climber as evidenced by his chapter on tricky placements. Randy tells us how to be sure a placement is good, and how to avoid a nasty fall. You will enjoy his stories, advice and techniques.

Jim Bridwell is Mr. Big Wall. His climbing career reaches back to the iron age, moves through the advent of clean climbing and into the 21st century. Jim accomplished the first one day ascent of El Cap; put up many El Cap classics like Sea of Dreams and The Pacific Ocean Wall; and continues to climb "pretty darn hard" routes today, like the Big Chill on Half Dome. Jim gives us a historical account of big wall climbing. Styles, ethics and people change. Jim shows us how these changes affect your big wall experience today.

Steve Schnieder followed in Bridwell's footsteps as a speed climber. He and partner Romain Vogler climbed two El Cap routes in a day, The West Face and The Nose. He has rope- soloed The Nose in 21 hours, 22 minutes and soloed the Direct route on Half Dome in 21 hours and 58 minutes. Steve gives us techniques for climbing fast, how to achieve a one- day ascents, and rope soloing. One of the freindliest guys you'll ever meet, Steve's chapters are filled with anecdotes and advice for any one who wants to push their big wall experience.

Steve Grossman takes the concept of clean climbing to the extreme. His concern for the climbing environment is reflected in his big wall achievements. Routes like the Jolly Roger and The Central Scrutinizer reflect a respect for the rock. Steve would rather run it out then place a bolt, work with the features of the stone, instead of creating placements. Steve writes about putting up first ascents and climbing ethics, two concepts that go hand in hand. For the ultimate fruition of any route is the second ascent and those who pass by in the future. Their opinion of what has been created matters far more than the achievement itself. Steve makes us think about the impacts all climbers have on the vertical world.

Then there is myself, your humble narrator. I bring the experience of a novice who has grown with each ascent. I can count the number of big walls I've climbed on my fingers and with each ascent I have gained a little more experience. I started with long routes like the East Butress of Middle Cathedral or Dream of Wild Turkeys in Las Vegas. Here I learned about climbing fast and climbing with efficiency. Next I tried The Washington Column and Half Dome and learned about hauling and living on the wall. Then it was climbing in the back country on Keeler Needle in the Sierra. I sampled different mediums, like sandstone, climbing a Zion Canyon trade route like Cerberus, before attempting a first ascent like The Equinox. As my experience grew, I felt confident about putting it out on the line. A one day ascent of Half Dome is possibly the finest experience a climber can have.

Then there have been failures. My first ascent on The Washington Column ended when my ninety pound partner realized he hadn't the strength or the weight to haul the bag. (By the way, this fellow is now an accomplished 5.13 climber). Or the time when I dropped the rack of pitons, only to have my partner catch them in mid flight. Shaken and nervous, I proceeded to drop them again! This time they hit the ground and the climb was over for us. How about the time on The Misty Wall when my partner crossed the haul line and the lead line. If he hauled and I followed, the two ropes would rub against each other, burning through, possibly unleashing me to gravity.

This book will help you avoid most nasty situations. Our collective experience will teach you how to be better prepared, keep the right attitude, and climb efficently and organized. The beauty in big wall climbing is that greater experience creates greater challenges. After completing a few El Cap routes, try climbing one in a day. Or take your skills to the back country and put up a first ascent. The ultimate expression of big wall competence is to put up routes in the big mountains where mountaineering, rock climbing and objective dangers keep you thinking. However, that's only after you've earned some experience. Hopefully, this book will give you some of the experience you will need to get started.

1. A BIG WALL

by Mike Strassman

"Rope is fixed!"
"Ready to Haul!"
"Haul Away!"
"Hauling!"

I am moving 200 pounds of water, food, climbing gear and beer to Sickle Ledge on El Cap. Dusk. Swallows play in the fading light. Tittering chatter mocking my exertions. My body is the counter weight pulling on the haul line. The haul bag scrapes up inches at a time. Its weight is caught by an inverted jumar. I stand up to repeat the process again.

It is my first El Cap route. The Nose. Half Dome and the Column are behind me. My partner, Sprague, is an engineer from Seattle. We barely know each other. We teamed up after I read a hand written note posted in a Seattle climbing shop.

Sometimes, that is the only way to get a partner. You feel the time is right and everyone around you is either inexperienced or has done the wall. After discussing strategy, I found Sprague to have comparable experience, a fun attitude and an intuitive mind. We were alike. We both felt ready.

I offer this narrative as an idea of what can be expected on an initial ascent of El Capitan. The Nose is the route of choice. Its continuous crack systems mean protection will always be available. You can concentrate on the climbing itself, instead of worrying about the potential for danger. The Nose has many ledges for bivouacs. That means you can take your time. It also has a bolted rappel route, making escape easy in the advent of injury or bad weather. Finally, it is a blast. The longest route you'll ever do. Three thousand feet of fun.

We had planned to do the Nose in five days, an average time. That translates to seven pitches a day. Someone who had recently climbed the Nose updated our topo map and gave us advice. Run pitches together on the Stoveleg Cracks, he said. Lower out farther than you think for the King Swing. His advice helped, but there were still many lessons to be learned.

As Sprague climbed onto Sickle ledge, I had a beer opened and waiting. We rationed ourselves to a six pack, leaving one a piece for the first three nights and none for the last nights when we would be more dehydrated. Planning was essential, even when it came to drinking beer.

We pulled sleeping bags from the top of the haul sack, pulled a gallon jug from the bottom, and unwrapped our ensolite pads from the sides. The stars appeared over Half Dome as we munched slightly warm chicken grabbed from the village right before we left.

Before going to sleep. I removed my contact lens. My first mistake. Big mistake. Glasses would have been a wiser choice. As the lens dropped from eye to hand, a gust of wind stole it away. I would be one eyed for the rest of the climb.

The next day, secure in our bags, we watched the morning sunlight descend the face. I was setting up the belay at the top of the Sickle when we were bathed in glorious light. Sprague carried and dragged the bag up the 4th class pitch, the easiest climbing on the route.

We felt energy pervade our beings. Honed after a summer of climbing, we felt competent in our abilities and enthusiastic about what lay ahead. Sprague set up the first pendulum, lowered out and swung over. He grabbed the crack on the first try. As he set up the next belay, I notice another climber appear on Sickle Ledge. We had another party on our tail.

"Rope is fixed!"

I began ascending the line to the pendulum point. By this time, I saw four climbers on Sickle, and two were already leading the 4th class pitch. I began to feel rushed. At the pendulum point, I clipped in and asked Sprague to tightened the rope to allow me to pendulum across.

"Don't you want to lower yourself out?" he asked.

I looked at the advancing climbers and at the smooth wave of granite across the pendulum.

"No," I yelled back, "I'm gonna go for it."

I unclipped from the pendulum point and started gaining speed. As I came around the wave, I realized that an unseen dihedral lay in my path. I was going to slam into it with devastating force. I threw my legs up in front of me and prepared for the impact. I hit hard, my knees absorbing the shock. I came to a stop.

Spraque stared in disbelief. "Are you all right?"

"Yeah..." I managed. My whole body was vibrating and the wind was knocked out of me. My knees hurt. Sprague probably wondered if he had picked the right partner for the ascent.

Second Mistake: Always lower yourself out when following a pendulum and don't allow yourself to feel rushed. It is better to take your time and do it right than make a mistake and lose your life.

Remarkably, I was unhurt. A little shaken, but ready to lead the pendulum into the Stoveleg Cracks. This pendulum defines fun. Instead of reaching for a hold at the end of the swing, you get a handjam. The most perfect jam in the world on the most beautiful crack you'll ever climb.

By the time Sprague had lowered out and swung across, the climbers behind us were beginning their swing. In no time at all there were six people at the belay. It made sense that all of us worked together to reach our respective bivouacs.

Unfortunately, these four climbers were German and did not understand a word of English. Certain words were universal. They knew "haul", "kletter" for climb, and "Bier". Let us kletter your ropes to haul and we will share some bier. We made our bivouac that night, but unfortunately missed the best freeclimbig of the Nose, the Stoveleg Cracks.

The German's tactics soon became evident. Wolfgang, was the head climber. He made all the decisions. Hans, was the leader; he led the pitches placing very little protection. The other two, Fritz and Ludwig were haulers. In their strange hierarchical way, these two climbers had to earn their way up the wall. Maybe later they could lead a pitch and next time, lead their own expeditions. The group's climbing style was remarkably efficient. The leading party fixed ropes for the hauling party. Since the leaders were freed of the hauling task, they could cover more ground faster.

The following morning was without incident. We followed the bolt ladder to the Boot, the amazing handcrack that separates Boot Flake from the wall, and the King Swing. But on the King Swing I did something not recommended. Instead of lowering the haul bag, I kicked it off. It tumbled free fall for 100 feet, caught and swung across the face. Although nothing happened to the bag, this can be a dangerous practice. When the bag catches, it puts incredible forces on the anchors. And, the bag might hit a ledge or the wall and burst, raining precious food and water on climbers below.

The King Swing, a double pendulum, was followed correctly. But, as follower, you are in a strange predicament. The second pendulum point is an ancient knifeblade piton, placed more than thirty years ago by Warren Harding on the first ascent. To follow this part, it is necessary to hang from the piton as you untie the rope to retrieve it from the first pendulum point. There you are 1500 feet up, resting on this manky old pin. In such situations always back yourself up by tying into the other end of the rope. However, if the piton was to fail, you'd take the King Swing like our haul bag did.

As we came closer to our bivouac for the night, Camp IV, we found the handholds covered in feces and dried urine. I was so disgusted that I used a skyhook and aid climbed instead of free climbing the 5.9 pitch. Going to the bathroom on the wall is uncalled for. Even the modern day method of going into a paper bag and throwing it off is beginning to wear on the landscape. The base of El Cap and its ledges are littered with paper bags that harbor an ugly surprise inside. With the amount of traffic these routes receive, I suggest that you take it with you. Bring a small bucket with lime in it to go in. However, this idea has not been received favorably by most big wall climbers with whom I've talked. Climbers enjoy the lightness of the haul bag as they approach the top. Additionally, there is the unappealing possibility that the contents may spill inside the haul bag. Yet, as more climbers tackle big walls, they must deal with this problem, and use a more environmentally sound method.

At Camp IV we found some other climbers had already made reservations. A Spanish team were pioneering a new route that merged with The Nose at that point. Camp IV is barely big enough for two people. "No problema" they answered and sped off down fixed lines. They spent the night on a huge ledge 150 feet below Camp IV while we crammed in the narrow perch.

From our vantage, we were treated to a horizontal moonrise. The wall was bathed in light. It was so bright, we felt as if we could keep climbing. Fatigue took over and we quickly fell asleep, feet dangling over 2000 feet of air.

The next morning we awoke to radio static and a heated argument in Spanish. These climbers had walkie-talkies to communicate with ground, and fixed ropes for the length of their route. Their ascent, The Mediterrane, was put up with siege tactics, as was the first ascent of The Nose. This weakens the sense of adventure, for if need be, they could return to the ground in a matter of hours. Rumor has it the climbers did return to the ground frequently and the route took the entire summer to complete. Compared to the commitment of a solo first ascent on El Cap, this route was a tourist's holiday.

We blasted off towards the Great Roof, one of the more amazing features on the route. Following The Roof, the climber must clip through the final pieces instead of jumaring horizontally (a dangerous proposition for the downward pull can twist the rope out of the jumars). Sprague found clipping into the fixed pieces to be just as dangerous. Each piece was looped with hundreds of pieces of old webbing. They began to rip through. I laughed aloud at his fear, knowing that I had him safe on a firm belay.

Sprague led the Pancake Flake, another excellent freeclimbing pitch, and I got the awkward aid pitch above it. The pitch begins with 15 feet of fourth class, and then a nasty flaring crack. I got one stopper half way in, then pulled up on it to get another placement. Suddenly, I found myself tumbling down the 4th class, hitting Sprague and launching into space. I tumbled upside down towards the ground wondering if Sprague was going to catch my fall.

I came to a back wrenching stop, peering at the Valley floor, three Empire State Buildings away. Sprague was screaming. I screamed back.

"Am I on belay? Am I on belay?"

"Of course you are," came the anguished reply. "How do you think I am holding you? Get up here quick!"

Grabbing the 5.11 crux of Pancake flake I laybacked up to the ledge. Sprague had rope burns over his forearm, where the rope had scraped during the fall.

We stopped. Let the hum of the Valley enter are senses.

Relax.

Too caught up in the act of climbing, we were not watching what we were doing. It was my mistake for not protecting immediately after the belay, and Sprague's mistake for not noticing it.

Adrenaline cleared our minds, heightened awareness.

Above us stretched the upper dihedrals. Such a pretty place to be. Planes of rock radiate away in perfect angles. You are climbing in the heart of a diamond. Now the stone brings you in. Every hold, every placement becomes an intimate realization. Amazed and aware we climbed towards Camp VI.

There were no more mistakes. A team of French climbers passed us at Camp VI. We let them climb our fixed rope on the condition that they fix a pitch for us. Stepping off of Camp VI we understood how overhanging the upper dihedrals are. I unclipped from the belay and swung twenty feet out. Dangling in space, I cherished these final hours on the wall.

The last pitch is a bolt ladder, drilled in the wee hours of the dawn by Warren Harding. Some bolts are missing, involving long top-step stretches in your aiders. If a bolt was to pop, you'd be helpless to continue further progress unless you had a bolt kit. We did not.

Hundreds of climbers have passed before us, and thousands will pass in the future. Each has felt the fulfillment of reaching this summit. A rounded bump perched on the rim of the Yosemite. Incomparable to the climb. We walked away, not talking, each silently reviewing the last five days.

It was almost night and we decided to walk down the Yosemite Falls trail instead of risk finding our way down the East Ledges descent. We walked in silence, awed by the experience that was behind us. There were more walls to climb, perhaps more mistakes to be made. Next time, the experience would be even finer.

2. LEADING TECHNIQUES

by John Middendorf and Michael Strassman

Big-wall climbs are a guaranteed adventure. You are dealing with a multitude of physical and mental challenges, all day, on technical rock for many successive days, setting up belays and bivouacs, and finally reaching the summit. This makes for an unforgettable experience. The unique state of mind achieved during multiple day big-wall ascents is so incredible that it is impossible to describe its essence on paper. Save it to say, that the motivations behind big wall climbs are more than just "because it is there"...

TECHNIQUES

The basic wall system generally requires three ropes: a lead line (11mm or 11.5mm), a haul line (9mm to 11mm), and a lower-out line (9mm preferred-optional for many routes).

Assume: Bert and Ernie on the "big stone".

1) Bert leads on the lead rope, Ernie belays.
2) Bert finishes pitch, fixes the rope (ties it into the anchor) prepares to haul.
3) Ernie releases haulbag from his belay (if need be, lowering it out with the lower-out line), Bert hauls it on haul line.
4) Ernie ascends the fixed lead line (Jumaring) and cleans the pitch.
5) Ernie arrives at Bert's belay, prepares to lead.
6) Ernie leads, Bert belays.
   Repeat until dark or until the summit is reached.

In big wall climbing speed is essential. For instance, it is faster for the follower to ascend the rope, than it is to free climb the pitch. It is better if the two climbers can accomplish two different tasks at once. So while the follower cleans the pitch, the leader hauls.

For experienced parties, climbing with three people can be a lot faster. Many systems are possible. After a pitch is led, one man will clean the pitch while the third man jumars a free- hanging rope. The leader hauls the bag. It is most efficient to have the person who jumared the free-hanging rope start to lead the next pitch while the previous pitch is still being cleaned. This requires a slightly larger rack. However, more gear can be sent up to the leader after the pitch is cleaned.

LEADING: GENERAL TECHNIQUES

Cleverness is an asset on walls; good judgement and innovative thinking are in constant demand. Besides the main challenge of a successful ascent, a wall offers a continual set of minor challenges, each one unique and each one requiring a slightly different solution. With experience, one learns the tricks of the trade. This occurs mostly through trial and error and the complex task of wall climbing becomes second nature. One develops an eye for a placement. The innate ability to deal with multiple ropes, slings, aiders, pins, biners, and an awareness of the interrelationship of the climbing gear, the stone, and upward progress.

While preparing for any lead, it is a good idea to first look at the line and devise a general plan. Consider how slings will be running as to minimize rope drag, or how, for example, a certain size piece should be saved for a latter section. Don't ever trust the topo, because it is merely a general guideline and by no means exact. Overall efficiency becomes the name of the game and accurate judgement is required.

GEAR

Proper organization of gear while preparing a lead is important. Utilize a system that gives you quick access and remains constant and familiar.

With double gear slings, racking can be both simple and comfortable. A possible arrangement: rack pitons (5 to 6 knifeblades per biner, 4 to 5 Lost Arrows per biner, 3 to 4 baby angles per biner, and 2 to 3 angles per biner), slings, and tie-offs on the right side; Friends, wire stoppers, copperheads, and hooks on the left side; and then distribute the free biners so as to equalize the weight on each side. How the gear is racked is a personal choice. Just be sure that it is always re-racked in the same place for maximum efficiency.

Let's start to lead.

As you place pieces, be aware of two things; how the rope will run once it is fixed and your partner is jumaring on it and how to best prevent rope drag. Be sure the rope does not run over any sharp edges and minimize traverses and rope drag by using slings.

If you are free climbing, place the piece to best protect yourself and the fixed line. But don't feel that you must adhere to a freeclimbing ethic. In big wall climbing, anything goes. If it gets tough, throw in a piece and hang on it. This is known as "french free" and may be used in more strenuous freeclimbing sections. If the climbing is really severe, start aiding. What ever is the fastest method is the method that should be used.

Know your freeclimbing abilities. If the topo says 5.7 or A1, it is probably faster to freeclimb; likewise, if the topo says 5.11 or A2 it is probably faster to aid.

AIDING

In aid climbing efficiency is important. You must be able to eye the placement accurately, place it, and move up onto it quickly. What takes up time is the problem solving involved in placement and the natural hesitation that comes with stepping onto a dubious piece. As you become more experienced at aiding, you will know how to place pieces securely, thus reducing the fear factor. However, you must be organized in your approach to aiding, with an efficient aiding system.

Aiding requires two aiders, a.k.a. etriers. Aiders are ladders constructed out of nylon webbing. They are clipped to the piece and used for climbing up and above the placement. It's nice to have a grab loop to steady yourself in the aiders and an extra second step to stand in with your other foot when moving one aider. For testing purposes, one of the two aiders should be longer: a 5-step instead of 4- step.

Two sets of two aiders can also be used. This way you can have both feet in one set, when moving the other set of aiders.

A daisy chain is a string of loops that connect the climber directly to the aiders. A carabiner can be connected to any of the loops for adjustability. Five millimeter perlon works well, doubled and knotted every foot or so. It should extend from the harness to the tip of your reach. The daisy chain should always be connected to each aider. It will retain the piece and your aiders if the piece should pull out.

Figure 2-1
Aiders

Figure 2-2
Fifi hook.

A fifi hook, an open hook, can be used for quicker connection and removal from the piece. The fifi hook helps take the weight off your feet and put it on your harness. It is nice to have a fifi hook on a short supertape sling (proper adjustment necessary) tied directly to the harness for quick clips.

To begin aiding:

a) place the next piece,

b) clip in the daisy

c) clip in a set of aiders,

d) test the piece,

e) get in the aiders and climb into the third step.

f) Hook in the fifi and hang from it.

g) After a momentary reprieve, decide what's required for the next placement, and climb up the aider.

h) clip in or back clean the last piece and repeat the process.

If you can, try and use the top step of the aider. Topstepping requires keen balance. If you are top stepping in a single step, you can place your other foot behind your topstepped foot to hold you in. Often, you can utilize holds on the wall for balance. This is known as "freeclimbing in your aiders". The daisy, clipped in short, can be used on overhanging sections to lever in a topstepping climber. A third aider may be needed because it is often difficult to retrieve the last aider while topstepping. In extreme situations, you can stand in the grab loop. In this case, the grab loop becomes the " hero" loop.

With the daisy, the rope doesn't need to be clipped into a piece until one is ready to move off it. This simplifies things and minimizes the potential length of a fall. Also, you don't have to leave in every piece that you have used for aid. By back cleaning a piece, you can reduce rope drag and save valuable pieces for later. Just be aware of your follower. On traversing or slanting pitches, back cleaning a piece might mean that the follower may have to take a swing between pieces. Also, be sure that you leave in the real bomber pieces to protect yourself.

When you are aiding a section that requires many pieces of the same size, you will want to leapfrog placements. This means that you clean the piece below you and place it above the piece you are standing in. This is easily done with camming devices, giving them the nickname "crack jumars". Again, be sure you leave a few pieces in to protect yourself.

One thing that you find is that aid climbing eats up biners. I find it best to never remove the biners from your aiders, always using free biners on pieces. After you have back cleaned a piece, remove the free biners and put them on your rack in an organized fashion. Adept use of slings will help save biners.

SLING USE

Slings reduce rope drag, save biners, prevent the rope from going over sharp edges, and equalize belay anchors. Carrying slings on carabiners on the rack, instead of around the shoulder, is quite convenient as it keeps them out of the way and fairly accessible. It also makes re-racking simpler, for the sling and biners function as a single unit, instead of three separate pieces. Twenty or 30 medium length 9/16" supertape slings, and 10 to 15 full-length 1" slings should be ample for most routes.

Be aware of sharp edges while on lead, both for yourself and for your partner who will be jumaring on those edges. Slings usually solve this problem, but infrequently an edge will be so bad that an article of clothing must be shed and left securely in place to pad it. You may consider bringing a two foot square piece of ensolite with a clip in loop for this purpose.

At belays, it's a good practice to equalize anchors with regular length 1" slings. Proper equalization distributes the load equally between two anchors, and is secure even if one of the two anchors should fail.

NUTCRAFT

Most A1 and A2 pitches can be climbed hammerless (without pitons) using only nuts, camming devices and wedges. However, when the time comes to place dubious placements, you must be able to make sure they hold body weight, and that you have protected yourself as securely as possible in the event of a fall.

Nutcraft is rapidly becoming a lost art. Some nut placements that you would not trust in a fall, will hold body weight. Nuts can be placed end-wise, or stacked between other nuts. A hammer tap may make a dubious nut placement more secure. If you can only get half of a slinged nut in, slide the knot of the sling up the exposed side of the nut and tie off the side that is wedged. All nut placements should be tested.

TESTING

There are two methods for moving onto dubious placements. In the ease-onto-it method, the climber slowly eases his weight off the present piece and onto the next piece, hoping it will hold full body weight. Then there is the more recommended shock-test method, where the climber bounces his weight on the next piece, slowly at first and gradually building up to forces exceeding body weight. Test with the aiders and daisy clipped in, not the rope. Of major importance, is preventing the piece you are standing in from getting shock-loaded if the tested piece does pull. This requires care. Properly done, however, most placements can be tested to handle a small shock load. Sometimes a dubious piece can't or shouldn't be tested, or can be mini-tested. For example long sideways placements, some roof placements and fragile hook placements; judgement is required. Testing in the midst of a string of dicey placements càn be one of the scariest parts of wall climbing.

Randy Leavitt will explain the intricacies of testing and tricky placements in another chapter.

A dubious placement is fairly obvious. Most small nuts, R.P's, H.B's, brass nuts, can only hold around 800-1000 pounds of fall factor. Sometimes you just can't get any conventional gear in and a piton will have to be placed. Often times a piton will make a dubious placement more secure. However, never place a piton unless conventional gear absolutely cannot be placed.

PITONS

Pitons are metal wedges that are hammered into cracks and holes. It has an eye for clipping a carabiner to it. Pitons are most commonly used in thin cracks, piton scars and as anchors in sandstone. They vary in size from small rurps to large bongs. Here is a quick summary of piton types from small to large..

Rurps: An acronym for The Realized Ultimate Reality Piton. These are thin pitons for seams. Rurps should be slung with cables, not slings.

Bird Beak: developed by Jim Bridwell, this is a rurp with a hook instead of a blade. The thin hook goes in where the blade won't, and hooks inside the seam.

Knifeblades: longer and wider than a rurp, a well-driven knifeblade will hold a short fall.

Lost Arrow: This piton is like a knifeblade, except the blade is shaped like a wedge for larger cracks.

Angles: Angle pitons are for cracks varying from 3/8" to 3". Most places you can get an angle you can get a camming device or a nut. However, they are used a lot for piton scars. But try and use something that you don't have to hammer in, even though a piton may feel more secure. Equipment technology has developed to the point that most angle placements can utilize a cleaner form of protection that doesn't destroy the rock.

Angles are also used for anchors in sandstone. A hole is drilled and the angle is placed inside it. **DO NOT REMOVE** these fixed placements, for it weakens the hole and a larger angle must be placed inside.

Bongs: Basically, these are large angles for 3" to 5" cracks. They are rarely used these days because camming devices do such a good job. Bongs have holes drilled in their sides to save weight. As they get older and rust, the bong breaks at these holes, rendering the piton useless and adding an ugly sight to the climb.

A

B

C

D

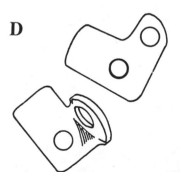

E

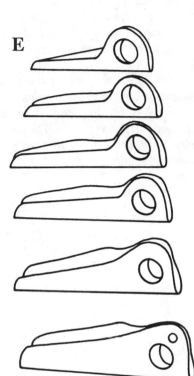

F

Figure 2-3 A-F
A.) Leeper Z-piton.
B.) Lost arrow.
C.) Shallow angle piton.
D.) Rurp.
E.) Angle pitons.
F.) 3" bong angle

Leeper Z : A couple of Leeper Z-pins are very handy to have on most routes. Although some people like to use them independently, Leepers can be stacked with an angle for a shallow or slightly oversize pin placement.

To place a piton, pick an appropriate size piton for the size of the crack. In time you will become better at this. Hammer it in with unrestrained force, but be gentler in sandstone or flakey rock. The piton will ring with each subsequent hit, starting with low tones and working up to higher tones. If you can make it ring all the way to the last hit, it is probably a secure placement. Do not over drive the piton. This makes the piton difficult to remove and damages the rock. If the piton stops ringing before you have reached the eye of the piton, and makes a dull tap when hit, you have bottomed-out or reached the back of the crack. A bottomed-out piton might still be secure if the tip is buried enough. In such a situation, you should either try to replace it, or tie it off and use it. Consider it a dubious placement.

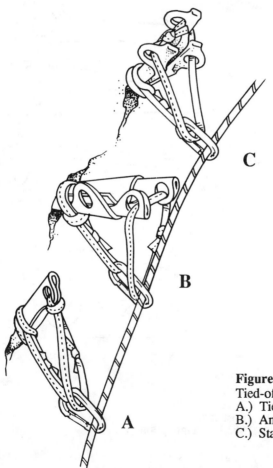

Figure 2-4 A, B, C
Tied-off pitons
A.) Tied-off piton.
B.) Angle stacked with a Z-pin.
C.) Stacked lost arrows.

TIE-OFFS

Tie-offs, short loops of 1/2" tubular webbing, reduce the leverage on pitons that bottom out. The sling is wrapped around the shaft of the piton at the clip in point. An overhand knot can be used to tie pitons off, but a clove hitch can be quicker and a lot easier to untie afterwards. A longer keeper sling, a tie-off looped through the eye and clipped in, will prevent losing the pin if it pulls out. Be sure the load is on the tie-off, not the keeper sling.

Pitons sometimes need to be stacked when additional tension for a placement is needed. Blades and arrows can be stacked, angles and Leeper Z-pins are commonly stacked, and large angles can be stacked with each other for placement in a large shallow hole. Tying a keeper sling, or regular tie- off through the eyes of the tied-off stacked pins minimizes the chance of losing them if they pull out.

OTHER PLACEMENTS

As one develops an eye for a placements, the best selection can be made from the arsenal of possibilities. Two-cammed Friends are often secure. They can be made even more secure by looping a nut around the buried axle and using it as the leverage point (body weight only). Brass nuts are frequently bomber in the bottom of pin scars. Bongs can be used sideways for large cracks. Placement possibilities are often endless for a given section of rock; good judgement will be helpful in choosing the most secure, most efficient placement.

Finally, overdriving pitons past the point where they are obviously bomber makes them very hard to remove and is usually unnecessary. It's that one last hit that transforms a pin from bomber to fixed. Avoid placements such as directly below a small roof where the pin will be unclearable, resulting in a geometrically fixed pin.

BELAY SET-UPS

Once the belay is reached, it is important to keep organized, as things become increasingly complex. As belays are set up, keep in mind where your partner will be coming up, where the hauling will be done from, and where you'll be hanging from while your partner leads the next pitch. When the anchors are spread out, belay set-ups are simple, but when the anchors are bunched together, proper set-up can be tricky.

Unlike free climbing belays, that may never be weighted, the Big Wall belay will see substantial forces placed upon it. You must be sure that the protection you place, or fixed anchors you use, are very secure.

If you are placing protection for the belay, spread the pieces out. Place the hauling anchors on the opposite side of the belay from where the fixed rope will run. There are two methods for clipping into the pieces. The safest, most bombproof method calls for equalizing all the anchors to a single point, and tying the fixed rope in with a figure eight knot to two or more carabiners. The disadvantage of this method is that it uses up a lot of gear and can be time consuming. The advantage is greater security in the event of a large load directly on the belay if the anchors are less than bombproof.

A quicker method, used when there are very secure anchors, utilizes a string of clove hitches to tie into the anchor. Clip each piece with two linked carabiners. Starting with the lowest piece, tie a clove hitch into the lower carabiner, tighten and tie another clove hitch onto the next highest piece, until all the pieces are linked by equalized clove hitches. Equalize the haul system on the higher pieces, clipping into the upper carabiners of each piece. Always clip any additional gear, belay seat, or porta ledges into the upper carabiners. This way, you never have weight resting on the tie in points of the rope.

Obviously, each belay is different, and may be aligned vertically, horizontally or spread out. The clove hitch method is safest in a vertical alignment, and weakest in a horizontal alignment. In the latter, all the force of the fixed rope is on a single piece. If in doubt, equalize the anchor to be on the safe side.

Tie yourself into the anchor with quite a few feet of slack to allow for hauling. Then clip your daisy chain closer into the anchor. (Clipping in with the daisy allows for you to disassemble the anchor, if the leader needs more slack on the next pitch.) Once clipped in yell to your partner below, "Off belay!" When the rope is fixed and ready to be jumared yell, "Rope is fixed!"

3. HAULING AND CLEANING

By John Middendorf, Steve Grossman, & Michael Strassman

HAULING

Hauling the bags can be one of the most strenuous activities on a wall. Warren Harding once refered to big wall climbing as "an excercise in vertical freight hauling." After your first multi-day ascent you'll understand why. It often seems that the majority of your time and energy is spent on this tiresome task. Actually, it is only a small portion of your time on a route, but it can be very unpleasant if not done efficiently. It pays to have a good system worked out, well before you get on the wall.

There are a variety of hauling techniques available depending on the relative weight of the haul sack. If it is less than your bodyweight a typical hauling system works as follows. The haul rope is fed through a securly anchored pulley. The slack is taken out of the haul line and an upside down ascender is used to prevent downward movement of the bag. You will probably need to hang some gear from the bottom of the ascender to keep it in position. A locking carabiner should be used to keep the gear from accidentally unclipping. The second ascender is used to pull the haul rope through the pulley. There are several methods of pulling on the second ascender. You can attach an aider to it and use one leg to push the ascender downward as it raises the bag. Or the secong ascender can be attached directly to your waist which allows the weight of your body to be used to oppose the haulbag. This is called Body Hauling. Body hauling is commonly used when hauling from a ledge or low-angle stance where the rope may be running over an edge and rope drag forces you to pull directly on the haul line with gloved hands or an extra ascender.

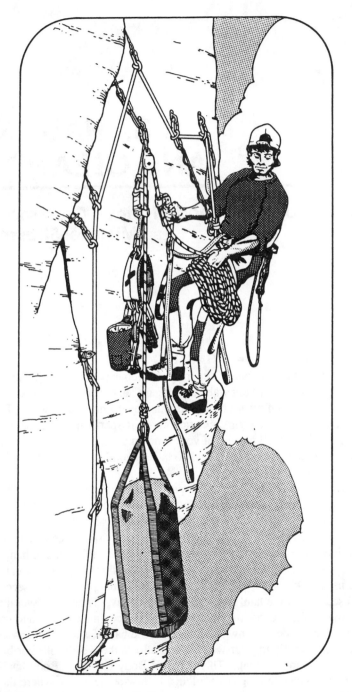

Figure 3-1
Leg hauling technique.

Figure 3-2
Body hauling.

Figure 3-3
Space hauling system.

Once the bag exceeds your bodyweight, counterbalance or "space" hauling is usually necessary. A pair of ascenders are attached to the haul line opposite the bag as if the hauler were ascending a fixed line. While loosely tethered to the belay with a third rope the climber uses full suspended body weight to counterbalance the weight of the bag. As with body hauling, gloves or an additonal ascender can be used to pull directly against the bag. Because of the substantial loads involved, the pulley should be backed up with a sling and doubled or locking carabiners in case it fails. If the hauling is truly heinous the second can help haul from the belay station. Multiple hauls or a two pulley system may be needed for light climbers or excessive loads.

When setting up a haul it is advisable to position the pulley off to one side so the haul bag does not crowd the belay. Once the haul system has been set up and the haul line is tight the leader yells, " Hauling!" and the second prepares to release the bag. If the pitch has been vertical then the second merely unclips the bag once the leader has raised it. He signals back to the leader, "Haul away."

If the pitch diagonals off to one side or is severely overhanging, the bag must either be lowered out or cut loose to swing. If there is any possiblity of the bag hitting the wall at the end of the swing it should be lowered out to avoid bursting water bottles or the bag itself.

There are many ways to unweight and lower the bag. The simplest is to clip or tie the end of a third rope to the top straps on the haul sack, run this rope through a carabiner above the bag and, using a belay plate, apply body weight tension to unweight and lower the haulsack.

However, if the diagonal is severe or the haul bag is too heavy, the unweighting step becomes more difficult. In this case you must set up a jumar assisted haul system and mini-haul the bag until its weight is off the anchor. Remember, always signal the leader that the bag is coming to avoid surprises.

Once the bag has been lowered out, it is usually a good idea to keep the end of the rope tied in. The wind can easily send a rope sideways to become irretrievably stuck. If the wind is severe the haul line may also need to be stacked during hauling to prevent snags or snarls. When in doubt take the time to stack the ropes and avoid a major headache.

Haul bags can easily get hung up on flakes or overhangs during a haul and become the source of considerable frustration. Usually the leader can see where the haul line is running and anticipate potential snags before they become a problem. If the bag becomes lodged, lower it a bit and try repeated tugs directly on the haul line to wobble it around the obstacle. If this does not work then you may have to wait for the second to dislodge it while cleaning or with the lowering line. Brute force sometimes succeeds but can also lead to cut ropes, torn haul sacks and time consuming bag retrievals. Try to be patient.

Once the bag arrives at the belay stance it should be clipped in with a sling and doubled carabiners to the haul bag straps. Some haul bags have a daisy chain securely sewn to the side which can be used to clip it in. This feature also allows easier access to the haul sack contents because the top straps are not un-

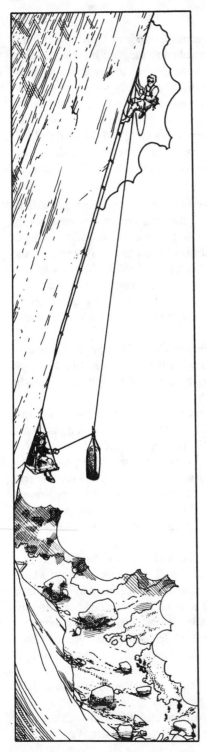

Figure 3-4
Lowering out a haul bag.

der tension. The bag should be positioned as high as possible to maximize the length of haul line available for the next lead. The haul rope should then be neatly stacked next to the bag. The haul straps can easily be used for stacking the haul line.

JUMARING

In the old days, fixed ropes were ascended using several prusik loops. A prusik is a loop of thin rope that is wrapped around the rope to be ascended. When weight is applied, the knot cinches down on the rope. To move upwards, the prussiks are loosened one at a time, slid up the rope, and retightened. The

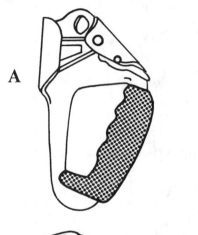

A

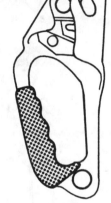

B

C

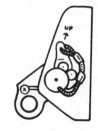

D

Figure 3-5 A, B, C, D
Ascending devices.
A.) Clog
B.) Petzl
C.) Kong
D.) Non-handled ascender

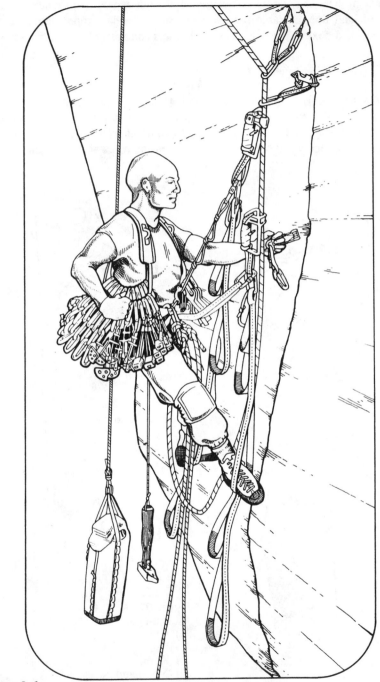

Figure 3-6
Cleaning a pitch.

climber is attached to the prusik by footslings or aiders and by a sling tied directly into the harness. The aider allows weight to be transferred from one knot to the other as the prusiks are worked upwards and the tie-in slings secure the climber to the prusik. Occasionally the climber may hang from the tie-in slings to rest. The system is backed-up by periodically tying into the rope.

Ascenders are the mechanical equivalent of a prusik knot. When weight is applied to the ascending device, a cam locks against the rope preventing downward movement. When weight is removed, an ascender easily slides upwards. You cannot move the ascender up when it is weighted.

It must be emphasized that these devices are specifically designed for ascending ropes and not holding falls or other loads in great excess of body weight. Whenever using an ascending device always have a back-up to the system. Never rely on an ascending device as your only means of safety. Ascenders can break or come off the rope accidentally. Always back yourself up by tying into the rope with a figure eight knot clipped to your harness and remain tied-in. Many people have died because ascending devices failed and they were not tied in. As with any piece of equipment, ascenders are subject to breakage or manufacturing flaws. They should be checked for wear and fatigue cracks, especially on the cam.

There are many types of ascending devices. Which one you choose is a matter of personal preference. The Jumar has become standard in Yosemite due to its straight forward ability to turn it into a hauling device. Like Kleenex and Xerox, Jumar has become a universal term to describe the technique and devices for ascending a ropeee.

There are other ascending devices. Clog ascenders have a wider grip, that allows for wearing mittens in extreme conditions; Gibbs ascenders are light and versatile, yet do not have a handle. They serve as an excellent third hand in rescue situations. The Kong ascender uses a leverage action, better for muddy or icy ropes. Petzl makes a chest ascender for ascending a free hanging rope.

Ascending the rope, also known as jumaring or jugging, can be done in a variety of ways. The most common method uses two daisy chains that are clipped directly from the harness to the ascenders. The daisy chain on the top ascender should be adjusted to the full extent of your reach. Also clipped into each jumar is an aider for each leg. Some climbers prefer a fixed footslings with a cinching footloop instead of an aider.

Before you ascend the rope, be sure that you are tied into it. Now slide the jumars up until all the stretch is pulled out of the rope. Stand in the lower aider and slide the top ascender up. Shift your weight to the tip aider and move the lower ascender up. Repeat the process. After you have ascended twenty feet or so, tie a figure eight knot as a back-up. Never remove the last knot until the other knot is clipped in. After tying in, you will notice that the lower jumar will not feed as easily. Manually pull the rope through the jumar until the weight of the excess rope through the jumar until the weight of the excess rope allows it to slide. After a while, you'll get the hang of it. A rhythm develops and you as-

Figure 3-7
Passing a piece while jumaring.

cend the rope smoothly, transferring your weight from one jumar to the other. However, if the fixed rope is overhanging, low-angle or sideways, problems may arise.

Low angle jumaring is difficult because there is a constant battle with rope stretch. Step up against the rock and the rope stretch is removed; pull on your jumar and the stretch increases. In these situations, remove your feet from the aiders and place the feet against the rock. You are effectively climbing with the feet and using the jumars for handholds.

In overhanging jumaring, there is a tendency to fall backwards. In this situation, clip the lower jumar close to your harness using the daisy chain, so you may rest on it. Move the top ascender up, stand in it, and quickly slide the bottom one up again. Rest on your harness when necessary. A striding motion can keep your weight over your feet and reduce the load on your arms.

Sideways and horizontal jumaring is dangerous. The rope can easily twist out of the cam. Whenever attempting a sideways jumar, ALWAYS TIE INTO THE ROPE! More than one death on El Cap can be attributed to this mistake. A carabiner can be clipped from the bottom of the ascender handle to the rope to keep the handle from torqueing on the cam as it moves along. In a sideways jumar it is sometimes easier to aid on the placements with an extra set of aiders, instead of using the ascenders. Use the jumars and tie-in knot as a back up. Always stay tied-in close in case the pieces should pull and you take a fall. Sometimes it may be easier to belay the follower on a traverse, provided all the placement are left in.

In any jumaring situation, do not bounce excessively because this may cause the rope to abrade or cut over an edge somewhere above. This should also be a consideration when the leader sets up a fixed line. Sharp edges can chop ropes and send climbers to their death.

There are times where you will have to remove the ascender from the rope to pass a piece of protection on a diagonal stretch, follow a pendulum or pass a fixed anchor. Always tie in or use a prusik before removing the ascender. NEVER UNTIE YOURSELF FROM THE FIXED ROPE! Be sure the lower ascender is weighted and your body is stationary when removing the upper ascender. Now place the upper ascender past the piece, making sure it bites the rope and slowly transfer your weight onto it. As the weight is removed from the lower ascender, the rope becomes slack, allowing you to remove the piece, or take the ascender off and pass the piece. As you weight the upper ascender the rope will pull the lower ascender against the piece of protection. Your gloved hand or a belay plate can be used to backtension this piece and allow the lower ascender to be unhooked and repositioned above the protection. Better yet, hold the cam of the lower ascender open as you transfer your weight, allowing the rope to slide through. Do not treat this situation lightly. Make sure those ascenders are firmly attached to the rope.

For example, notice Figure 3-7. Before the climber weights his left jumar, he should tie closer into the rope. When he weights the left jumar, it will pull on the right jumar. To adjust for this, he will hold the cam of the right jumar open and let the rope slide through, until all his weight is on the left jumar. Then he will clean the piece, and slide the right jumar up.

There may come a time, such as when ascending or descending a fixed rope, that you may not be able to tie into the rope. A prusik must be used as a back up, or another line as a belay. Never ascend a fixed rope without a back-up to your ascenders.

CLEANING

Efficiency while cleaning is a must. Keep removed gear organized while cleaning a pitch. This makes re-racking for the next pitch simple. As you clean, try and rack the gear as it would be for leading. Disassemble biners and slings from gear to form two separate units. Group together nuts or pitons of the same size on a single biner. If the gear is organized when you reach the belay, the gear transfer will be accomplished quicker and smoother.

PITONS

For cleaning pitons, I usually sacrifice a large sturdy biner. Clip the cleaning biner into the piton to be cleaned and to a sling that is clipped into you. This prevents the piton from being dropped and allows some leverage to be applied. Now hit the piton on the sides, back and forth along the axis of the crack, until the piton starts to come out. At this point, the piton can be levered out with the pick of the hammer, jerked out with the cleaning biner or removed by hand.

In newer placements it is best to hit the piton in a predominently upward direction. This creates a v-shaped piton scar that may allow for a nut to be placed there in the future. This technique is known as constructive scarring, and is particularly important in softer rock.

PENDULUMS

The simplest, quickest and safest way to clean short pendulums is by lowering yourself out on the fixed rope. First, make a bight or loop with the end of the rope you are tied into and pass it through the pendulum point sling. Now, clip the bight into a biner attached to the harness and pull the slack out of the bight so your weight is on the bight and not on your jumars. Unclip the pendulum point biner, and lower out. Once you have reached a position where you can start jumaring vertically, attach the jumar to the fixed line and unclip the bight from your harness. Now pull it through the pendulum point. Don't forget to tie the fixed rope in close to you, before pulling the rope out of the pendulum point.

If there is not enough rope to lower out on, a third rope may be substituted to lower yourself out. Just be sure you are tied into the fixed rope.

TRANSITIONS

Making the transition from cleaning a pitch to leading the next pitch can be one of the more awkward times on the wall, especially when the belay is cramped. A well set up belay, with anchors spread out as much as possible, makes transitions simpler. Efficiency is the key.

The gear should be ready to go with little re-racking. If the leader and follower have their own individual gear slings than re-racking is less involved - as long as the follower cleaned efficiently. The haul and lead ropes should be stacked away from each other and running freely. The "spaghetti management system" where everything is left to hang and tangle at will is not recommended. Instead, careful organization and separation of the various ropes will save time and energy. Different colored ropes allow for quick identification. Stacking a rope through a sling or using a rope bucket, keeps it from blowing around and getting tangled. Be sure the leader has everything he will need to set up the next belay and haul. I find it best for each climber to carry his own pulley instead of transfering a single pulley. This leaves a back up should one pulley be dropped accidently.

Once the leader has all the gear he needs, jumars for hauling and a pulley, he is set to go. Always place a protection piece immediately after leaving the belay. If the leader should fall, the force will be on the piece, not the anchors. Be sure that the haul line is running freely and pay attention to the leader's needs.

Sometimes the leader will need additional gear sent up from belay while leading a pitch. He can haul it up on the free- hanging haul line. This is not a problem if less than half the rope is out. But if more than half is out, the haul line will have to be untied from the haul bags, and the lower-out line attached. This is a pain-in-the-arse. Too avoid this situation either make sure that you have everything needed to finish the pitch as you near thc half-rope point, or use a zip line. This requires an extra rope. On harder routes, trail a 7mm zip line instead of a haul line. Besides being lighter, gear can be sent up easily at any point on the pitch. At the end of the pitch, the zip line is then used to pull the haul line up.

THE BELAY

Hanging belays can be uncomfortable. Sitting on the haul bags is an option to a butt bag. If you are belaying a long aid pitch, you may want to break out the porta-ledge (See Chapter 4). The porta-ledge set up makes for luxurious belays. Or, a comfortable seat can be fashioned out of a two-foot square piece of padded plywood with two holes drilled in the corners of one side, and one hole drilled in the center of the other side. Rig with slings. The center sling should be adjustable. On The Central Scrutinizer on El Cap, Jay Ladin rigged up a lawn chair into a belay seat for the ultimate in comfort.

These items can be hauled outside the bag if necessary.

Always be attentive on belays. Sometimes a hard aid pitch may take most of a day. It is easy to space out on the passing clouds and birds. Always have a hand on the rope and perhaps a knot backing you up. Be aware of snags in the rope, and the needs of the leader.

Some climbers bring a paperback book along to keep them company. This is alright, but should not get in the way of upward progress.

"Watch me, this looks dicey."

"Wait 'till I finish this chapter!"

FIXING

Fixing the first few pitches on walls is standard practice. Without making the full commitment, the initial work can be done on the wall. Fixing can also be used when you have reached a good bivouac ledge and want to establish a high point for the next day. If possible, fix station-to-station. Otherwise, ropes can be tied together and left to hang. As mentioned, try and fix halfway anchors for maximum safety.

Leaving gear on the wall lessens the eventual work load, but watch for gear thieves, the lowest form of life. Actually, this hasn't been too bad a problem in recent years, since getting caught could and should be fatal.

Now you understand how Bert and Ernie made it up the Big Stone. But what happens when they needed to go to the bathroom? Where did they sleep? Is it true that climbers bring cold beer on wall climbs? For the answer to these and other questions, turn the page.

4. LIVING ON THE WALL

By Mike Strassman and John Middendorf

ATTITUDE

Big-wall climbing is a sport in itself. An adventure requiring specialized gear, specialized techniques, and above all, a specialized state of mind. In fact, the state of mind required for a multi-day big wall ascent is so unique that many are unable to click into it. Thus the initial failure rate by far exceeds the initial success rate.

Commonly, a climber's natural impulse, once on the wall, is to immediately want to go down. If the mind succumbs to this impulse, it then rationalizes reasons for not being there. Consequently, many parties retreat without any specific reason, but with stacks of general ones: weather looked poor, not enough water, forgot I had a dentist appointment. Generally, if it's possible to push through the first day or two of indecision, the rest is easy.

A determined and positive attitude is required for a successful big-wall ascent; dispassionate or negative attitudes guarantee failure. Big-wall climbing requires concentration. The ability to keep it together for long periods of time, combined with forethought and a fine-tuned awareness of the environment. You must have commitment. Commitment towards achieving a goal, and a willingness to repeatedly make an effort and deal with hardships positively. Above all there must be communication. The ability to work effectively and efficiently with partners. These mental aspect of big-wall climbing can be just as challenging as the physical aspect.

Be prepared physically. Most climbers like to train for big walls by climbing. Climb some long routes with your partner and become familiar with transitions, speed, and communication. Climb often, with appropriate rest days, so that you are in tip top climbing shape. Although some out of shape people have pulled off some amazing ascents, climbing fitness is important. You should be able to climb 5.10 solidly and be able to climb 10 moderate pitches in a day.

Everything you will take with you will fit in the haul bags. You can man up, and take a bare minimum of supplies for a lighter speedier ascent. Or bring everything you'll need and treat the wall as a pleasure cruise, taking a maximum amount of time to complete the ascent. Let's face it, big wall climbing is rough enough; you might as well be comfortable and enjoy it.

FOOD AND WATER

A stove is impractical to bring on a wall. So your food should be canned or bagged. Come up with inventive meals; it's better than beans out of a can. Always have plenty of treats, such as candy, cakes, juices, and nuts. These little niceties put a smile on your face when things aren't going well.

Water is an important consideration. One gallon per man per day is minimum. You want to be able to stretch out your water if trouble arises. Many walls seemed to end with the climbers rationing water to the last drop.

The classic method of carrying water is in thoroughly cleaned gallon jugs for bleach. These are protected with thick layers of duct tape. A string keeps the top attached to the bottle. A sling is thread around the handle for clipping the jug in.

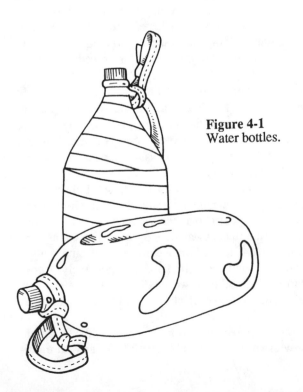

Figure 4-1
Water bottles.

Two to three liter soft drink bottles are virtually indestructible. A sling can be duct taped under the lip, and a keeper sling attached to the top. The one advantage these bottles have over gallon jugs is that if they should blow out, they will not lose as much water.

SLEEPING

If you are fortunate to have a large ledge on the route, you may forgo the weight and bulk of a porta-ledge. However, porta-ledges are far more comfortable than a cramped ledge. A porta-ledge is like a cot that can be folded up for hauling. Another alternative is a hammock. Although they are light and compact, they are not very comfortable. If you climb a ledgeless route and use a hammock or porta-ledge, know how to set it up before you get on the wall.

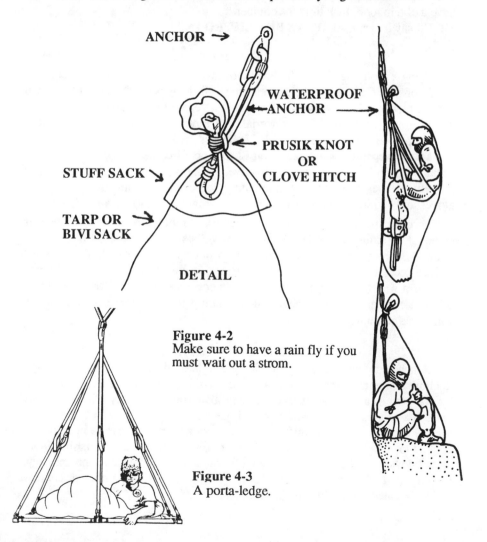

ANCHOR →

WATERPROOF
← ANCHOR →

STUFF SACK ↘

← PRUSIK KNOT
OR
CLOVE HITCH

TARP OR →
BIVI SACK

DETAIL

Figure 4-2
Make sure to have a rain fly if you must wait out a strom.

Figure 4-3
A porta-ledge.

A porta-ledge with a rain fly can keep you very dry if you must wait out a storm. Be sure the seams of the fly are coated and that water cannot enter the fly. One problem is water seeping in through the tie-off point. To avoid this, put a nut inside a stuff sack and tie a prusik around the sack and the sling of the nut. Feed the end of the nut's sling into the fly and clip the ledge to it, with the stuff sack covering the flies opening. Clip the ledge into the nut and the prusik into the anchor. Be sure you are clipped in!

If you are climbing a route like The Nose or Half Dome, there are adequate ledges for bivys. Ensolite pads can be wrapped around the inside of the haul bag for padding, then removed at night for sleeping. Although down sleeping bags are lighter, they don't retain warmth when wet. A synthetic bag is a better choice. Your sleeping bag, pads and anything else you have on the wall should have a clip in loop. Including the climber.

I'll say it again. **ALWAYS BE CLIPPED IN!!**

CLOTHES

Bring everything. Most climbers know what they need to survive extreme conditions. El Capitan can be a sweltering 100 degrees or cloaked in snow and ice. Be prepared for adverse weather with a layered clothing system. Do not use cotton, down or nylon. These materials are ineffective when wet. Gore-tex, Polypropelyne, wool and other wickable fabrics are key.

Some exposure related deaths on El Cap occurred because climber's hands became numb with cold and ineffective. Bring two sets of gloves, a poly-propelyne inner and gore-tex outer mitt. Some climbers are using neoprene gloves and booties, like divers use, for the ultimate insulation against dampness.

There are special clothing you will need for climbing. A pair of knee pads is essential for aiding. Fingerless gloves, like cyclists use, keep the gobis to a minimum. A helmet is mandatory. One dropped piton can kill you. A hat under the helmet keeps the sun off the face. For shoes, use a comfortable rock climbing shoe or a wall boot. Forget bringing your neon rock slippers. You want something that is comfortable enough when standing in slings, put can still friction when free climbing.

ADDITIONAL GEAR

A headlamp with back-up batteries and light bulbs is a must. You may have to climb at night. A first aid kit is also required. Duct tape is the universal repair kit for your gear. A speedy stitcher may also come in handy. A Swiss army knife is a universal tool as well as a wall spoon.

Be careful with your knife around a tensioned rope. Pressure need not be applied to cut a tensioned rope. Once on a retreat, a fellow caught his shirt in his rappel device. As he cut it free, the knife touched the tensioned rope and snip! Luckily, he had placed a nut as a back up. However, it was a poor placement. and he sweated profusely while awaiting a rescue.

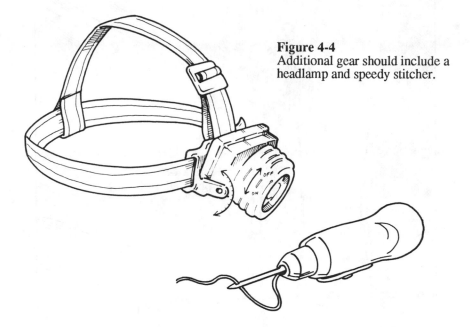

Figure 4-4
Additional gear should include a
headlamp and speedy stitcher.

OPTIONAL GEAR

A walkman or boom box is nice for those who like to break dance on their porta-ledge. Beer can be easily hauled. Freeze your water bottles and place them around the beers to keep them cold. Drink only at the bivys, not while climbing.

PACKING THE HAUL BAG

Make sure water bottles, especially on lower angle routes, are well padded with duct tape or ensolite. It is best to have the water bottles on the bottom, below the sleeping bags, in case of breakage. Certain items need to be handy such as extra rack, plus food and water for during the day. Rain gear should also be accessible, so pack accordingly. A day-pack or a pocket in the top of the haul bag makes organization simpler.

Organize items in the bag with stuff sacks. I usually have a food bag, sleeping bag, clothing bag, ditty bag, butt bag, old bag, etc. The bags can be easily clipped in and out as needed.

The haul bag should have its own daisy chain for clipping it in, as well as a tie off loop on the bottom for carrying another rope. The bag will suffer a lot of abrasion so be sure it is packed streamline with no unsightly bumps and bulges. You can protect the haul bag knot by cutting the top of a bleach bottle off, threading it through the haul rope and covering the knot. You may want to bring a haul sheath, a covering of ballistics cloth, in case you need to haul a pack, or your haul bag develops a hole.

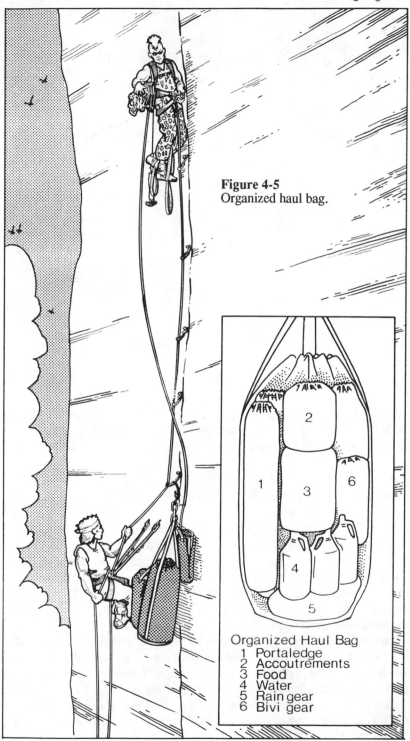

Figure 4-5
Organized haul bag.

Organized Haul Bag
1 Portaledge
2 Accoutrements
3 Food
4 Water
5 Rain gear
6 Bivi gear

A haul bag should have an expandable inner sleeve that extends the bag to six feet in length. You may have to sleep in the bag should you lose a sleeping bag. It happens!

CLIP IN

As you will discover, living on the wall is a perpetual process of clipping things in and out of anchors. The simple task of handing a water jug to someone becomes complex.

"Gimme the water."

"Let me unclip it. Here you go."

"Thanks."

"Got it?"

"Got it." Clip.

With so much clipping and unclipping, you may get confused, and accidently unclip the wrong thing. A lost haul bag, rope or sleeping bag might mean the end of your big wall adventure.

After I accidently unclipped the rack of pitons on an attempt of Timbertop Mesa in Zion Canyon, we decided to retreat. We would not make it to the ground that night, so we bivyed on a ledge partway down. I counted our remaining pitons and decided we still had enough to complete the ascent. I discussed it with my partners. They wanted to go down.

"I am not worried about you unclipping the rack," my partner confided, "I am worrying about you unclipping me."

The next day we descended, depressed and distracted. I was the last to leave the ledge and clipped into my rappel device. I went to unclip from the anchor and... I was already unclipped! I was perched a thousand feet up off belay!

STAY TIED IN AT ALL TIMES!!!

GOING TO THE BATHROOM

The traditional method has been to go in a paper bag, and throw it off. However, with increased traffic, the base of El Cap has begun to smell like a sewer treatment facility. I know a climber who was hit by one of these stink bombs. It exploded all over his ropes and gear, ending his ascent.

Going on the wall is even worse. There is nothing more repulsive than climbing through feces.

May I suggest a new method for the ecological conscious '90's. Bring a small bucket, similar to those used for storing bulk foods. Be sure it has a lid. Put some lime in it and bring it with you. Be sure the lid is on tight and that the bucket is padded.

Urination is easy for guys; the stream quickly evaporates in the air. For women, it is more difficult. A pee bottle may be used to keep it off the route. Dump it at a place where it will quickly evaporate in the wind without hitting the wall.

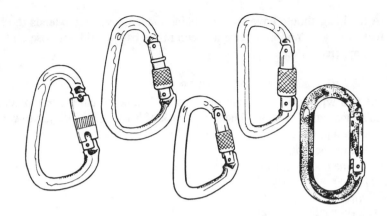

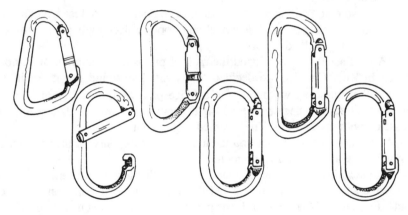

Figure 4-6
Various types of carabiners.

RETREATING AND RESCUE

It's always a good idea to keep in mind a general plan for emergencies. Weather can be a major cause of trouble on walls; proper storm gear, even in the warmer seasons is a must. Check the local forecast before attempting a route. Know the local signs of approaching weather, such as, high cirrus clouds, change in wind direction, etc.

There are many things that can go wrong in a big wall climb. What would you do if your leader has taken a fall, is unconcious, with more than half a rope length out? Figure it out. Think about different possibilties and how you would get out of it.

Self-rescue is the preferred escape method. Calling for a rescue should be avoided unless absolutely necessary. Keep in mind that a rescue is never a simple task. Rescue personnel have died trying to reach stranded parties.

In Yosemite, there is no charge for rescues... yet. However, if poor preparation is a factor in your rescue, the National Park Service may charge you with negligence. Many cases have already been brought to court. Big wall climbing is not like sport climbing. You are on you own out there.

If you decide to retreat, keep these things in mind. Retreating is difficult on steeper routes, usually requiring down-nailing. Sometimes pushing on may be easier. How secure is the anchor? Leave gear behind if you are unsure. Where is the next anchor? Try and locate it before attempting the rappel. Always knot the end of the rope and have a pair of jumars with you should you not find the anchor. A prusik is nice as a back-up when rappelling. If you are retreating in damp, cold weather, be aware of hypothermia.

During a storm, we discovered that our belay was in the path of a waterfall. My partner sat in the torrent while I rappelled. By the time he reached the ledge, he was shivering uncontrollably. He rappelled to the next ledge and placed the anchors. When I arrived and inspected the anchors, I found them to be unacceptable. When I asked him to explain, he babbled incoherently. Hypothermia reduces the flow of blood to your extremities, including your head. Be careful. If hypothermia is suspected, terminate your retreat and work on getting warm.

Also be aware of other natural dangers. Rock fall is common in storms. Lightning will electrify a stream of water or strike the face itself. In sandstone and softer rock, drilled anchors may weaken. If you are soaking wet, watch the air temperature. If it drops below freezing, you can quickly turn into an ice cube. Change your clothes as the temperature reaches freezing.

Don't play hero. There have been some amazing self-rescues, like Doug Scott crawling out of the Himalaya with two broken legs. I know a fellow who broke his arm, splinted it with his nut tool, and rappelled to safety. Accidents bring shock to the body. You may not be functioning rationally. Call for a rescue if bones are broken or there is massive bleeding, but not for a sprained finger.

Hopefully, you will never have to be rescued. Living on the wall is just too much fun to have it spoiled by such an ugly occurrence. But accidents can happen. Be prepared, keep aware, and have a good attitude. And STAY TIED IN!!

5. BIG WALL CLIMBING HISTORY

By Jim Bridwell

ED. NOTE: We are pleased to have Jim Bridwell as contributor to this book. His big wall adventures exceed those of the other authors. Jim has been climbing since the Golden Age of Big Wall Climbing, and has taken a lexicon of techniques to distant corners of the planet. He has climbed some of the most massive walls in the most extreme conditions. In this chapter, Jim explains how technique and gear developed. An in-depth look at gear will follow in the next chapter.

1930-40

Climbing big walls began, naturally enough, in the mountains of Europe. After the major summits were conquered the sheer and often overhanging faces of the Alps and Dolomites were next. They held a magnetic attraction for extremists. As early as the 1930's, the Comicis and Cassins attacked the Dolomite walls with hundreds of soft iron pitons, well suited to the twisty cracks and holes of the limestone rock. These pitons were left in place for future ascensionists.

1940-50

A lull in climbing persisted during World War II. Metal for gear was scarce, and young climbers were needed for the war effort. However, some important technical developments emerged - the nylon rope and aluminum carabiners. Another important advancement was the hard steel alloy pitons invented by John Salathe, the father of American big wall climbing. John, a blacksmith by trade, had fashioned the pitons from Ford axles. Unlike their soft iron predecessors, these were durable pitons that allowed for removal and repeated use. Fewer pitons were now required for a big route and the level of commitment rose. In 1947 Salathe made the first ascent of Yosemite's Lost Arrow Chimney with Ax Nelson. Attention shifted to America with its superb craftsmen and idyllic sun bathed walls.

The equipment manifesto had been issued. Increasingly, developments in big wall climbing depended on improvements and innovations in equipment. Lighter gear and durable pitons were landmark advancements, but they were just the foundations of what was to come. Chromemoly pitons became available to the public as did improved aluminum carabiners. Walls that seemed unclimbable, now lay within climber's grasp.

1950-60

The stable weather and sound rock of Yosemite made it a mecca for big wall climbing. A small group of dedicated hardcore climbers, the "Californians", began to practice the big wall art. The prize was the Northwest Face of Half Dome. This fell to Royal Robbins and crew. Next, siege was set on El Capitan's Nose by Warren Harding. Unlike Robbin's quick, self contained ascents, Harding opted for an expedition style of ascent. Ropes were fixed for long stretches as the climbers pondered the puzzles of the wall. The wide cracks on the Nose presented an unusual problem to Harding. He cut legs from stoves to fill the gap, creating the forerunner of the Bong piton. Long blank stretches were over come with many expansion bolts. Three years later, El Cap was climbed. The ascent combined technology and determination to overcome what many considered unclimbable.

Although Robbin's set the tone on style, with continuous ascents and a minimum of bolts, big wall climbing was still a formidable task. A system for hauling the ponderous loads of food, water and gear, was needed. Equipment was still primitive, with greater variety needed to fit the myriad of possibilities. Siege climbing was the practical method of doing the big routes and bolts overcame obstacles. However, many developments in equipment came out of this era. As with the stovelegs for wide cracks the knifeblade was developed by Chuck Wilts to penetrate thin ones. It is interesting that during these formative years in Yosemite the metal rung etrier never caught on and was universally renounced in favor of the soft nylon webbing aiders.

1960-70

This was the "Golden Age" of Big Wall climbing. It was a time when necessity became the mother of invention. Soon the rurp was created by Tom Frost to stem the malignant growth of bolting in the early 1960's. These Realized Ultimate Reality Pitons could be placed in bottomed, rotten seams where other pitons were found unsatisfactory.

Similarly, the lack of stances and ledges ushered in an array of ingenious ac-

Bolt Bag contents:
• Spare drills

• Drift pin and/ or
  wrench

• Hole cleaner
  (blow-tube)

• Bolt selection

Figure 5-1
A traditional bolting
technique with aid.

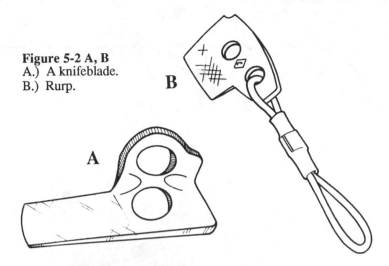

Figure 5-2 A, B
A.) A knifeblade.
B.) Rurp.

cessories that made hanging out more comfortable. The belay seat and the hammock found ready acceptance. Royal Robbins, after a productive visit to Europe, solved the load hauling dilemma. He used the newly acquired Swiss ascender, the Jumar, in a unique way.

Utilizing body weight in combination with a pulley the Jumar could hold in place cumbersome haulbags. By the middle of the 1960's technology had all but eliminated siege tactics. The North American wall, and shortly after, the Muir wall, stood as testimony to elegant style.

Later in the 1960's two innovations, the hook and quick or shallow hole aid device, made their debut. Both have become standard big wall gear. Soft iron ring-angles, bent over, served as the first hooks. A 1/4" rod of aluminum mushroomed at one end placed in drilled holes became what was known as a dowel. The dowel would hold only body weight and therefore would not sustain a fall. An early attempt on the Dawn Wall saw the first use of these on a big route.

During this period, the humble haul bag evolved from a rudimentary army duffel to the high tech portmanteau.

Figure 5-3
Old ring-angle claw.

1970-80

This era witnessed intense activity on Big Walls throughout the world as well as many dramatic developments in equipment. Big wall techniques and technology had started to change climbing in remote mountain areas. European climbers, as well as Americans, were using places like Yosemite as a training ground for progressive projects in Alaska, Patagonia and Baffin Island.

Climbing on the walls of Yosemite underwent a transformation. With the major cracks systems climbed, attention shifted to piecing together discontinuous cracks and flakes, with hooking and shallow hole drilling.

Machine bolts driven into the shallow hole soon replaced insecure aluminum dowels. Warren Harding invented the B.A.T. (Basically Absurd Technology) hook. This was placed on the edge of a drilled hole. Climber's now drilled their way up the walls and came under stern criticism from their peers. Such was the case with Warren Harding's Wall of The Early Morning Light. Taking over 28 days, this route was a monument to innovative route finding and technique. However, many felt the wall had too many bolts, and Royal Robbins chopped many of the bolts on the second ascent. But as Robbin's climbed higher, he found the climbing to be demanding and brilliant, regretting his destructive action. Thus was born the first climbing ethics controversy - a controversy that continues today.

Various manufactured hooks of chrome molly were made available. Yvon Chouinard once again lead the way. Chouinard, always the innovator, began the nut revolution in the early 1970s. Aluminum wedges known as "stoppers" and "hexcentric" were created especially for the subtleties of Yosemite cracks. These stemmed the growth of ugly piton scars generated by repeated placement and removal. An array of sizes and shapes soon competed for the market including the incredible crack'n'up for the smallest cracks. The new rage was "Clean" or "Hammerless" Climbing and many major routes were done using only nuts.

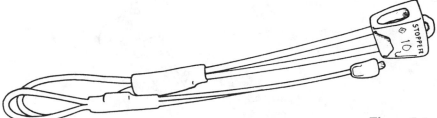

Figure 5-4
Stopper.

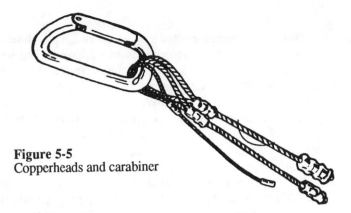

Figure 5-5
Copperheads and carabiner

Just after the aluminum nut was the introduction of a simplistic gadget by Bill Forrest, the "copperhead". This revolutionized hard aid climbing more than anything since the piton. It virtually eliminated the craft of difficult shallow pitoning.

In the mid seventies there was a quantum leap in hardware technology with the camming device. Born of the genius of Greg Lowe, these little (and big) babies took the bite out of everything from overhanging hand cracks to most expanding flakes. The sliding nut, though older in concept, was adapted to a functional form at about the same time. The "slider" could be used in thinner cracks but lacked the integrity of the opposing cams of Friends.

If severely sustained and difficult aid routes were the fashion of the seventies, comfort was also the mode. Mike Graham's collapsible sleeping cot, the Cliff Dwelling, made it possible to get a reasonable nights rest. This enabled climbers to maintain the energy and drive necessary for extreme routes devoid of natural ledges. A rainfly was added and security complimented hedonistic opulence.

Figure 5-6
Friend

It seemed that the "Big Wall" climber was turning into a self indulgent Prima Donna, missing the pluck of generations afore. In instances this was true, but concomitant to a few of these types were those who took this technology to the harsh conditions of the great mountains. In Patagonia, Pakistan, Baffin Island and Alaska, walls that before bordered on insanity now came under the canopy of the plausible. The envelope was stretched on routes such as Fitzroy, Cerro Torre, Trango Tower, Uli Biaho, Asgaard and Mount Thor.

1980-90

What else, you might enquire, could be gleaned, garnered or added to this panoply of paraphernalia? Not much, but man, like nature, abhors a vacuum and therefore a few items of note filtered their way into the ever growing regalia deemed essential to the hip aid specialist. The trend tended toward bigger and smaller additions to gear available. Smaller camming devices the T.C.U., Triple Cam Unit, found acceptance as did larger opposing cam gadgets. A spring loaded, locking, tubular contraption the "Big Bro", all but reduced offwidth cracks and squeeze chimneys to docile diversions for not-so-adept free climbers. Some other useful and novel tools that have been recently introduced are: the Bird Beak, manufactured by A5 adventures. This combines the concepts of a rurp like piton with a hooking function. A slider nut by A5, called the Monkey Paw, appears at this time. It is perhaps the most sound of its type. Two software items were introduced by Yates, an adjustable sling for a clip-in on ascenders and an impact reducing tie off for tenuous aid placements.

New big walls became scarce in frequented areas and few independent lines were ferreted out. Routes began crisscrossing or using parts of other routes. The big walls of remote regions beckoned with the promise of adventure. Significant climbs were done in the Baltoro towers of Pakistan, huge walls on Baffin Island, mountain faces in India and the tempestuous Torres of Patagonia.

The Future

With the popularity of sport climbing, many activists will infiltrate the sanctuary of the technocrat, big wall climber. An ever widening cross section of participants will crowd the walls. Many who read this book will be wrapped in the adventure of unraveling the arcane mysteries of big wall logistics. Meanwhile the avant garde will be exploiting and perfecting skills to push the borders of the impossible in hostile environments, at higher altitudes and in more remote locations. Paradoxically old skills may be neglected. The profusion of modern technology is not just useful but now essential. Complex gizmos are no substitute for resourceful ingenuity when survival is the reward.

The Rating System

It is of interest in this historical sketch to identify the changes in form and method for rating the difficulty of aid climbing. In America, prior to the late 1960s, when the A1-5, European system was first introduced, we used a decimal system similar to the free climbing rating of this country. Categorically 6.0 was the easiest and 6.9 the most severe. This system was unnecessarily complex and the European method found immediate acceptance.

Initially A1 was a perfect crack that was neither strenuous nor reachy and awkward. A2 was a good crack but awkward and strenuous. A3 would require more difficult placements that couldn't be counted on to sustain the impact of a fall. The upper end of the scale, A4-5 got a little sticky as to what was what. It was generally accepted that A4 was one to three aid placements which would hold body weight only, but a definition of A5 was not universally agreed upon. Two theories were offered. One that A5 is just more A4 in a row, or the other that two placements equally weighted were necessary to hold the climber's body mass. Initially, the former method was more used since the latter seldom came into play. Around 1974 the novel idea emerged - that a potential 60 foot fall constituted A5.

This opened a Pandora's box. The overt egotism of a few self ordained experts decided that a 100 or 150 foot fall constituted A5 and that A5+ was a possible death fall. This rating system is totally absurd since someone has to die before this rating applies.

Late in the 1980s, in answer to the continuing perversion of aid ratings, a very general, simplistic and somewhat humorous rendering was offered using letter abbreviations: N.B.D. meaning, No Big Deal, would cover all easy aid. N.T.B. stood for Not Too Bad, the middle ground. P.D.H. stands for, Pretty Darn Hard, and would apply to all difficult aid climbing. Although this system says all that needs to be said about difficulty it says nothing about the seriousness of a pitch. So R.H.U. or, Real Heads Up, was added to supplement any of the other ratings.

This system, though somewhat frivolous seemed nonetheless practical and comprehensive. But apparently not so. On the first test route using these ratings, the second ascent team, insecure with new concepts, reverted back to the A1-A4 equivalents. This of course, negates the whole idea.

Ed. Note: So much for C.R.S. a Casual Rating System.

6. GEAR

By John Middendorf

GETTING STARTED

Big walls are gear intensive, but it is possible to get started on the big stones with an moderate amount of additional gear. Two climbers each with a standard free- climbing rack and decent camping/bivy gear have all the gear for most Yosemite trade routes and about 2/3 of the total gear needed for a moderate aid route like Mescalito, Zodiac, or the Shield. For the latter routes you will need pitons.

PITONS

The wall will determine the amount of hardware required. If the route has had more than ten ascents, the gear-list given in the Meyer's guide to Yosemite should be modified. Continued piton placements expand the piton scars. The Shield is an extreme example of beaten-out cracks. The route used to rely heavily on smaller size pitons such as knifeblades, rurps, and lost arrows; now it demands more medium sized pitons like 1/2" and 5/8" baby angles and 3/4" standards. In some placements you don't have to hammer the piton at all. Hand-placing a 5/8" angle in what was originally a knifeblade size crack is not uncommon. It is advisable to have some sawed-off 3/4" and 1" pins for shallow pin scars so the piton will not bottom out. One or two of each should be sufficient.

This does not detract from the overall beauty of the route. With innovations in gear, these piton scars can be climbed hammerless. Intricate use of tri-cams, sliders, and similar hardware adds a new challenge to the ascent. As a rule, climbers should try to use hammerless protection on routes like the Shield to protect the rock from excessive scarring.

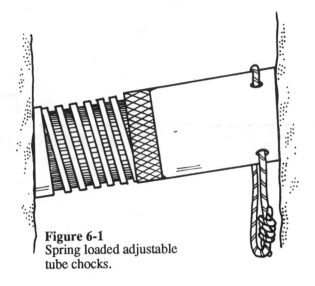

Figure 6-1
Spring loaded adjustable
tube chocks.

With the advent of camming devices fewer large pitons are required. But on routes where the wide-crack predominates, such as Excaliber, bongs are a necessity. A bong may be wedged with a block of wood in larger cracks.

For most nailing routes, three to five 1" pitons, two or three 1 1/4" pitons, one or two 1 1/2" pitons, and a bong for luck will generally suffice. This assumes that you have a good selection of camming devices. Take two or three of each size, plus an oversized camming device.

A wall changes with each ascent: pieces get fixed, placements become more obvious and simple, loose rock gets removed. Walls become easier with use and the gear-lists change accordingly. Consult the topo or someone who has recently ascended the route for specific gear requirements.

"When on the big stones, make sure you're tooled up to the gills." - Jim Gaun

HOOKS

Familiarity with the various hooks, also known as sky hooks, and a knowledge of how they can be used is essential. Practice on the boulders, preferably not the chalked ones, to get a feeling for hooks. When hooking, always keep a daisy connected to the hook/aider so it doesn't blow away or become lost in case of a fall. Bring extra hooks because they're frequently dropped.

There are three types of hooks: the Chouinard, the flat and pointed Leeper

Logan, and the ring-angle claw. The Chouinard hook is the most common. For some routes, such as Zenyatta Mendata, pointed Chouinards are necessary. File down the end of the hook into a sharp point. Imagine a 45 degree triangular point. These hooks are used in enhanced hook placements where a shallow 1/4" hole has been drilled in a horizontal or sloping shelf to allow the hook to catch.

Leeper hooks are essential in some situations. The flat-Leepers are very stable and secure on narrow edges where a Chouinard hook would rock. Very frightening. On thin low-angle slab climbing, a filed flat-Leeper is useful. The pointed-Leepers also have other uses. They work great for bat-hooking. A bat hook is used where a drilled hole is the only placement. The hook grasps the edge of the hole. Sometimes a slight tap with the hammer sets the hook nicely. But beware, if you pound them in, they can spring out suddenly.

Ring-angle claws are named for the type of piton they were made from. Years ago, one would have to search desperately for a long, soft-iron, ring-angle piton and bend it to the proper shape. The ring angle claw is an enlarged version of the regular hook. Professional models such as the FishHook are now available. These hooks are essential on some routes, Their uses range from hooking large, two-inch-thick detached flakes to hooking a large solid shelf. For some routes, several sizes may be required.

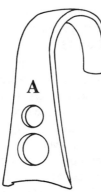 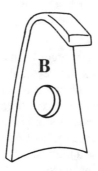 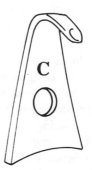

Figure 6-2 A, B, C
A.) Chouinard
B.) Leeper flat hook.
C.) Leeper pointed hook.

COPPERHEADS

Copperheads or mashheads are specialty big-wall items. These are mashed into shallow grooves or pockets as aid placements. The copperhead is a piece of metal, a swage, that is pressed around a cable. They are often handmade, or may be purchased pre-made. If you're worried about quality, buy a Nikkopress

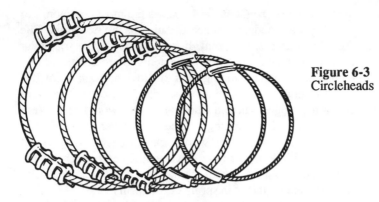

Figure 6-3
Circleheads

gauge for a couple of dollars and make sure the swage meets sizing specifications. This will guarantee its strength. Also make sure that the doubled-back wire just peeks out of the swage. If it comes out too far, it will fray and catch on slings. You can also make your own with a swager. A swager crimps the metal around the cable. The heads will cost thirty cents each in materials, but a good swager will cost $150.

The sizes of copperheads range from #0, about 1/8" in diameter, to #5, about 1/2" in diameter. The #0's have a cable that will just about hold a gymnast. They aren't used much. The #2, #3, and #4 are used more often . An adequate rack for a typical El Cap nail-up would be 2 #1's, 8 #2's, 6 #3's, 5 #4's and 3 #5's

Aluminum is often used for the larger heads, #3 and up. They are more secure than their copper counterparts. However, alumniheads are not very durable. They may only survive one or two placements before they become useless.

Copperheading is an art, learned through experience. A tool is frequently needed for placing the smaller heads. For larger copper or alumiheads, the pointed end of the hammer is often effective. Lost Arrows pitons work okay for placing copperheads. Personally, I use a blunted 5/8" chisel. The chisel is strictly for use on the copperhead; never for enhancement of the rock. For most placements, the old" X-em, paste-em, rock-em, sniff-em" technique is adequate. X-em: hit the head with multiple cross-hatched blows; paste-em: pin the right and left side in; rock-em: hit the top and bottom and watch to see if it "rocks"; and finally, sniff-em, and "if it stinks, get off it!".

To remove a copperhead, connect a sling from the copperhead to the hammer. A hole in the hammer head simplifies this. Swing upwards, jerking it out. It is a considerate practice to leave a copperhead in place if it looks like the wire will rip out. Otherwise, an unsightly blob of metal would remain in the only spot the placement can be made and must be tediously cleaned out by the next party.

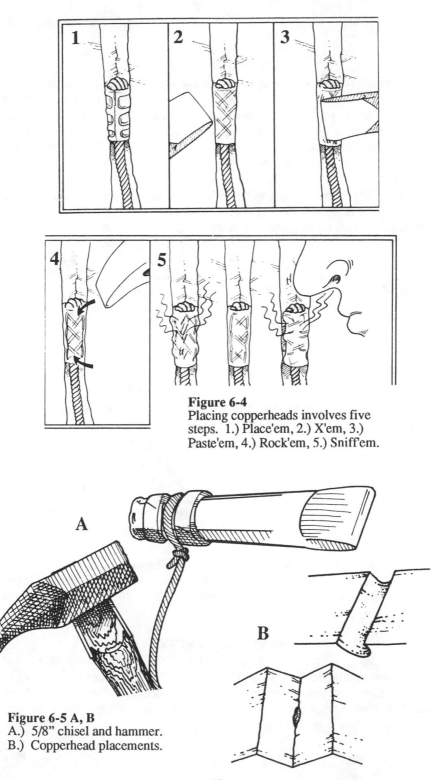

Figure 6-4
Placing copperheads involves five steps. 1.) Place'em, 2.) X'em, 3.) Paste'em, 4.) Rock'em, 5.) Sniff'em.

Figure 6-5 A, B
A.) 5/8" chisel and hammer.
B.) Copperhead placements.

BOLTING GEAR

A small bolt-kit is nice to have for any route of medium or harder difficulty. It can be used for replacing a bad belay bolt, setting a bivouac rivet, or drilling emergency anchors for retreating. On established routes, a bolt should never be placed as protection where a bolt did not previously exist. A couple of 3/8" drill bits, drill holder, drift holder, drift pin, and a few 3/8" bolts with hangers should be ample. Smaller size bolts may be brought in case of emergency, however, belay bolts should always be replaced with 3/8" or larger stainless steel bolts. Some routes, such as Never-Never Land, that have hangerless bolts at the belays, bring five or six hangers. Also include some 1/4" course-thread nuts and a wrench for hangerless threaded bolts.

RIVETS

A rivet is a 5/16" diameter, 3/4" long, coarse-thread, grade 5 machine bolts that is hammered into 1/4" holes. They are body weight placements that will not hold a fall. A rivet does not have to be drilled as deep as a bolt, thus saving the first ascentionist time and energy.

Figure 6-6
Rivet hanger--for body
weight only.

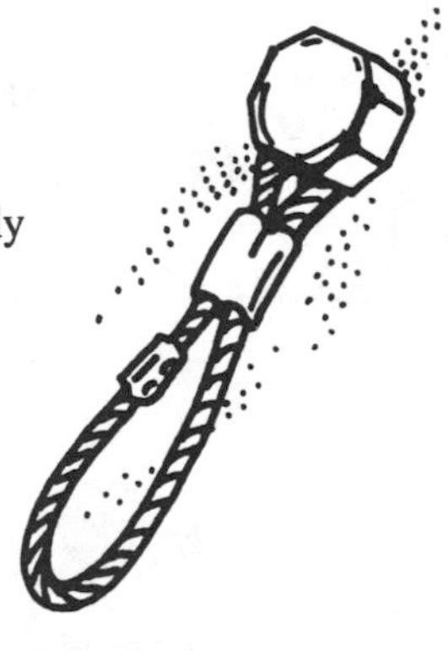

RIVET HANGERS

Wired stoppers work well as rivet hangers. Simply push the nut down the cable and slide it over the rivet. One-half inch tie-off sling also works. For shorter length rivets, specially-made rivet hangers can be fashioned out of a swaged wire loop (see diagram).

KEYHOLE HANGERS

Keyhole hangers resemble a regular bolt hanger, except they have a key hole so they can be fitted over a bolt-stud, such as a Rawl buttonhead. They can be made from any hanger simply by filing a connecting slot from the carabiner hole to the bolt hole. Australian RP-type hangers work well as keyhole hangers for the larger head machine bolts.

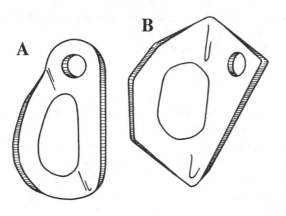
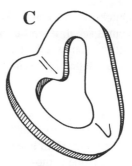

Figure 6-7 A, B, C
A.) SMC hanger.
B.) HME hanger.
C.) RP Keyhole hanger.

FREE BINERS

Free biners are any biners that are not used for racking purposes. It seems one can start a pitch with a ton of free biners and still be forced to scarf biners from other parts of the rack. There never seems to be enough. A total of 50 carabiners is needed for easier routes, 80 carabiners is a minimum for most nailing routes, extreme routes may require up to 150.

CAMMING DEVICES

Camming devices are indispensable on walls. They are probably the greatest energy-saving device ever invented for wall climbers. The ease of placement and removal speeds things up considerably. Two or three sets are nice to have on most walls. More may be needed depending on the nature of the wall and the amount of leapfrogging a climber is willing to do. Half-sizes are handy, too. More than two #4's are rarely required.

CHEATER STICKS

Though some consider cheater sticks unethical, they are all part of the game. A cheater stick is a long stick used for reaching past placements. A fifi hook, carabiner, or sky hook is placed at the end of the stick, with a loop of sling reaching down to the climber. The climber hooks the next placement, instead of dealing with the placement that is before him. Some climbers feel that it's just an extraneous piece of gear that gets in the way. But on some of the newer routes, such as Lost in America, cheater sticks are required for sporty hooking past blank sections.

MISCELLANEOUS HARDWARE

About thirty wired stoppers and hexes of various sizes, and at least two or three sets of brass nuts down to #0 are an adequate "wired" rack for most routes.

Quickies, slider nuts, TCU's, tri-cams, and HB nuts are good items to have in your arsenal. Even hexes, those rarely seen funny shaped things from the stone age, can be useful. It is a good idea to have a great variety of gear. Sometimes a certain type of gear may be the only thing that works.

ROPES
Always, the lead-line should be in good shape. Walls tend to be harsh on ropes, especially while going over edges and being jumared. 11.5 mm ropes are comforting. Haul lines are less critical. Either a 9 mm or an 11 mm can be used. A static line is most efficient for hauling because there is not any stretch. A third line can be used as a lower out line, a zip lines or as a second lead line.

All ropes should be the same length - no less than 165 feet long.

In sandstone, be especially careful over edges, even rounded edges. The rope will wear a groove in the rock. A small piece of ensolite with a clip in loop will prevent this from happening.

TIE-OFFS
Depending on the wall, anywhere from 10 to over 100 tie-offs may be required. Tie-offs get trashed on some placements, such as when tying off a piton in a corner. One-half inch tubular webbing is standard. Loops ranging from five to seven inches in diameter seem to be the most versatile.

SLINGS
Many slings are required to keep rope drag to a minimum. Also use slings to equalize belay anchors. Form 9/16" supertape slings into quickdraws instead of carrying them around the neck. Tie these a little shorter than regular length runners. These slings can be doubled through the eye of a piton, thus saving a carabiner.

FALL ARRESTS
These are slings that are sewn together with bar tacks. If the sling is severely loaded in a fall, the bar tack breaks. This absorbs the shock before the piece does. Surprisingly, Air Voyagers and other fall arrests haven't really caught on in wall climbing as much as they deserve. They can be reassuring on that relatively secure but somewhat dubious piece in the midst of a long string of body-weight placements.

PULLEYS
An efficient pulley is essential. The red or blue SARA rescue pulleys are very reliable. Always bring a spare pulley, Once, I dropped a pulley and for the remainder of the wall had to haul through a carabiner, expending a thousand times the effort. Self camming hauling pulleys are available, such as Rock Exotica's Wall Hauler. These are incredibly convenient devices. You don't need to rig a jumar into each haul system. Be sure to bring two pulleys, just in case.

HAMMERS

An A5 hammer, with its hefty weight, copperheading pick, and carabiner hole is the recommended big-wall hammer.

HAMMER HOLSTERS

A soft hammer holster is best because it doesn't dig into your flesh during belays and bivouacs.

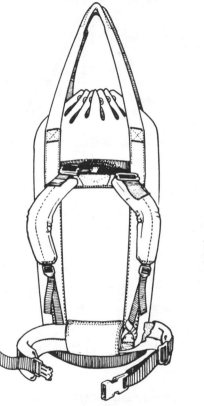

Figure 6-8
Haulbag.

HAUL BAGS

Many types of haul bags are available. Make sure that the material is both tough and abrasion resistant. A haul bag should have a padded carrying straps and waist strap for the approaches; a pocket or top flap for quick access; an inner sleeve; a daisy chain or tie on loops. I've always found that the stout, wide haulbags were far easier to get in and out of and pack than the long, narrow ones.

A haul sheath is nice for hauling a pack or in case the haul bag develops a hole.

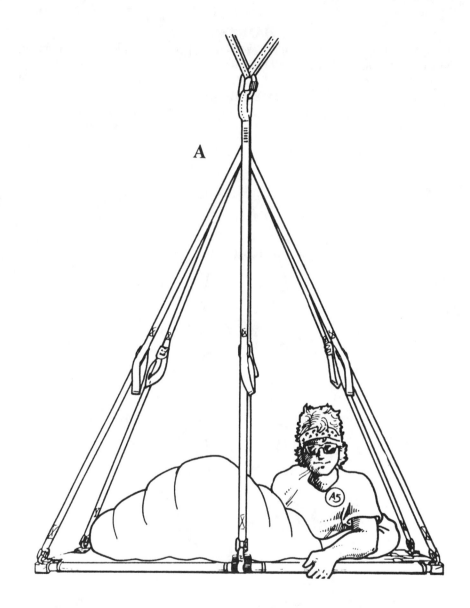

Figure 6-9 A, B
A.) One man portaledge.
B.) Two man portaledge.

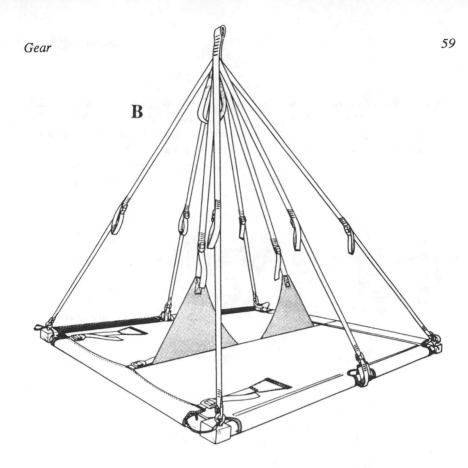

B

RACKING SLINGS

Without a doubt, the double-gear sling is a great innovation for heavier gear loads. No longer is the climber strangled by gear-slings crisscrossing his neck. Instead, two padded slings on each shoulder connect in back and front. The most versatile racking slings have two loops on each side for maximum organization and strong tie-in loops for clipping the entire rack in.

PORTA-LEDGES

There are many types of porta-ledges on the market. Some are excellent, some are poor. Porta-ledges should be easy to set up, lightweight, and roomy enough for lounging. A good porta-ledge will be stable. It should not twist, hourglass, or parallelogram. This requires rigid corner sections. A porta-ledge should be easy to adjust while sitting in it. But many of the adjusting systems slip, especially when wet, causing the entire ledge to twist out of shape. This piece of equipment could mean the difference between survival and death in a severe storm. Be sure it works.

A good heavy-duty rainfly is essential. Practice setting up the whole system in your backyard with the hose spraying it. You will need to be prepared for the worst.

FOOD

A matter of preference, of course. For a five-day wall, I would typically take five or six cans of dinners (lasagne, spagettios, beans, etc.), three or four cans of fruit, a box of Familia to mix in with the fruit (breakfast), four or five packages of bagels and cream cheese, a couple packages of Fig Neutrons, and a selection of candy bars. Make sure to get the sealed-wrapper type. Some hard candy are also good to keep your mind off water while sitting at belays.

Figure 6-10
Harness.

HARNESSES

You will hang in a harness most of the day. A comfortable harness is a luxury. A wide waist harness of 4-6 inches with gear loops, and well padded leg-loops makes for a good harness. The leg loops should be removable for going to the bathroom and changing clothes. A tie-in harness is preferable to a buckle harness for safety. Either way, a locking carabiner should be used to clip the harness to the rope, in addition to tying the rope into the harness. As a final back-up, tie a sling around your waist, and clip the locking biner and rope through it. Don't forget a belay-seat of some sort.

AIDERS

My favorite are the sewn, rigid-step, four-step aiders. Especially if it's windy and the aiders spend half the time whipping around your head. It's nice to have a rigid opening to throw your foot into. I use four aiders; two on each biner. Aiders can also be knotted from one inch webbing. These have the advantage of being custom designed to your body.

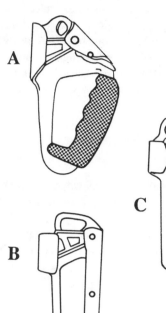

Figure 6-11
The are three main types of ascenders.
A.) Clog
B.) Jumar
C.) CMI

ASCENDERS

There are three main types: Jumar, Clog, and CMI's. The CMI's are the strongest, but you need the fingers of Houdini to work the triggering mechanism. Jumars and Clogs are easier, and more comfortable. It's all a matter of preference.

HEADLAMPS

Headlamps are essential for setting up a bivy in the dark. The preferred headlamp fits entirely on your head without a separate battery pack. Besides getting caught on everything, the wires invariably have a built-in instinct to strangle. The best headlamp is the Petzl Zoom with the 4.5 volt flat European type alkaline battery.

SHOES

If you are climbing a wall with a lot of free climbing you will want a comfortable pair of all-around climbing shoes. However, if you plan on climbing mostly aid, Robbin's wall boots are still the standard, but unavailable. Any shoe can be used, but a wall will demolish most tennis shoes. A good lightweight hiking boot is preferred. The Nike Lavadomes are incredibly durable. I have a pair that's survived four walls. These shoes also have a semi-rigid sole for comfort in the slings. Resole with climbing rubber for the ultimate wall boot. A comfortable pair of free-climbing shoes for the occasional free-climbing section is a good option. Tie-in loops strung through the eyelet is convenient for clipping in your shoes at night. If you drop your only shoes, you can kiss your feet goodbye.

KNEE PADS
Nice to have because knees are constantly battered on walls.

GLOVES
Gloves are a must for protecting hands. I only use them while cleaning a pitch. The thin, tight-fitting leather goat-skin glove with the fingers cut off above the first knuckle are the best.

Taping your hands will also protect from abrasion. This is a nice option if you are climbing a wall with a lot of jam cracks. Even while aiding, you may need to sink a jam for balance.

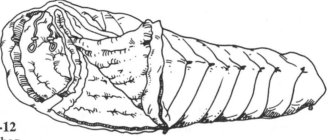

Figure 6-12
Sleeping bag.

SLEEPING BAG
Synthetic insulation only. A wet down bag could kill you. A Gore-Tex bivouac sack will provide additional protection should your porta-ledge blow out. A clip-in loop sewed on to the bag is nice.

RAIN GEAR AND EXTRA (WARM) CLOTHING
Use wickable and breathable fabrics, such as polypropelyne and gore-tex. Avoid using cotton or down, as these do not retain warmth when wet. A neat set of rain pants are made by Mountain Hardware. The Grade IV Rain Pants can be slipped over your harness. They have a velcro opening that allows the rope or carabiner to be passed through. A wind shirt is also a nice item to have.

BASIC BIG-WALL GEAR CHECKLIST

Hardware (SFG stands for standard free-climbing gear) 2-3 Sets of Friends (SFG) 2-3 sets of wired stoppers (SFG) 2-3 sets of small brass-nuts (SFG) 80 carabiners (SFG) Hook selection (2 to 5 of the standard types) Copperhead selection (10-25) Pitons (5-10 knifeblades, 10-20 Lost arrows, 15-25 angles) Small bolt kit (optional)

PERSONAL WALL GEAR (PER CLIMBER)

Harness* Aiders* Ascenders Hammer & holster Headlamp Helmet Rain gear Wall-boots* Kneepads and fingerless gloves Wall spoon and Swiss army knife Sleeping bag and ensolite

OTHER STUFF

Haul-bag* Portaledge* Double gear sling* Ropes (2-3) Tie-offs and runners Pulley (2) Stuff sacks for gear/food organization Water Bottles Accoutrments, inc. speedy stitcher and duct-tape Food First Aid Kit

The items on the checklist marked with an asterisk are subject to improvisation; a portaledge, for example, can be anything from a plywood sheet rigged with cord or a suspended K-mart lawn chair to the deluxe, manufactured portaledges now available. The harness can vary from a simple 2" swami and 1" legloops to a custom made padded wall-harness. Aiders can be knotted from 1" web, or sewn. A duct-taped duffel bag may suffice as a haul-bag, or regular back-packs can be used to haul gear. A good, well-manufactured haul- bag maded from abrasion-proof materials, however, is worth the investment. Two gear slings can be sewn together for and adequate double gear sling.

This is by no means a complete gear list. Decide on your specific needs according to the wall you are climbing. It is always better to take too much, than to take too little. Just be prepared for the worst, even if it may seem like overkill.

7. TRICKY PLACEMENTS

By Randy Leavitt

The granite wall bulges above, an imposing wave frozen at its most threatening moment. I strain my neck to look at the belay, a mere thirty feet away, but onc more hour of climbing. The rock is firm and compact with features small and perfect - a Japanese garden. The sum of its tiny parts create the huge expanse of El Capitan, the testing ground for America's aid climbers.

"A perfect medium for aid climbing", I ponder as I strain to look at the belay once again. It mocks my position, which is tentatively fixed on a skyhook behind a hollow flake. The flake moans and creaks. I've been on similar flakes and know this one probably won't pull off. I shudder to think of the consequences: you simply can't consider falling at the end of an A5 pitch. Above, I find the only placement is a knife blade behind an expanding flake. This feature is so thin that I fear having to use it...

The overhanging wall cuts below me revealing only my last 40 feet of tiny copperheads mashed into a thin, blank dihedral. They would never hold a fall. But 80 feet down I remember placing a solid Friend below the roof. I hang onto this memory with agony. I am almost to the safety of the belay above. Sweat pours off my forehead and stings my eyes. August on El Cap is hot. Five minutes...I need just five minutes...to hunch over, hang by my harness and try to relax while suspended by a hook. I need to think and rationalize.

THE FLAKE SNAPS!!! and I prepare for the 150 foot fall! No... it was just the carabiners shifting. I want a drink. I want a bolt. I rationalize just one more placement.

I remember the knifeblade and the flake above. I select a long, thin blade to drive into the unknown space behind this fragile flake. The blade drives easily, much too easily, so I decide not to use it. Immediately above, I place a larger piton, a Lost Arrow. The flake resists its entry. I pound harder and smash my knuckles in the struggle. The useless knifeblade falls out as the flake expands. I am mesmerized by its fall. It slices the air and reaches terminal speed, then starts to tumble before it hits the trees below.

Back to reality, I clip up to the Arrow and apply bodyweight. It holds, so I bounce on it lightly. It holds this test so I bounce furiously. The piton snaps downward at an acute angle but doesn't come out. My heart races towards cardiac arrest. I ease back down onto my hook and hunch over for five more minutes.

My position is serious, so I take my time. The flake is too expanding for pitons. It has expanded nearly all the way without breaking. I realize that a very small nut would work where the knifeblade fell out. I place it, test with bodyweight, lightly bounce, then heavily bounce. Another piece of the puzzle is in place. I am now 83 feet out from the solid Friend placement, and only one more hour needed to cover the last 25 feet to the belay. Then, eight more days of this to the top!

Big wall aid climbing is an incredible and delightful puzzle. Each experience fits together to form the adventure of a lifetime. This chapter is about "tricky" aid placements. How you get in and out of exposed situations. This is the most enjoyable and rewarding part of wall climbing. The continual problem solving. The actual climbing constitutes only a small percent of tricky aid.

TESTING TRICKY AID

Aggressive Testing. This is the key to surviving long sections of dubious aid placements. I learned this art from a real pro named Dale Bard. I was aghast watching Dale bounce furiously up and down on very marginal placements. "What if that piece came ripping out?" I asked.

Dale explained. "Assume that you test each placement in this very aggressive manner. You can be confident that any piece along a string of bad placements will hold this type of force. If a piece pulls out during an aggressive test, your last placement should hold the force of the fall." It may not hold much more than that. If the piece has been tested incorrectly, and it rips out, it will generate more force on the piece below it. This could zipper out the entire string of placements. Tricky aid is risky. Just be sure that the last piece can withstand a sudden weighting of your body plus a small amount for dynamically applied force.

Aggressive testing works like this. Make the placement above and clip your free set of aiders (a pair, two on one carabiner) into the top piece. Next, clip one of your two daisy chains into the carabiner that holds your top set of aiders. If this is too high, clip your daisy chain into a lower loop of your top pair of aiders.

You may be tempted to clip the rope into the top piece. Do not. Clipping your rope into the top piece accomplishes nothing except to make your belayer do more work and lengthen your fall. Your daisy chain will keep you and your gear attached if the top piece pulls out. .

Get ready to begin the test. For dubious placements, test in the lower rung of the aider. If the piece pulls out you will be level with the lower piece, minimizing the length of the fall. If the piece is more secure, you can get higher in the aiders to save time. However this risks more force being generated on the bottom piece if the top one pulls out.

Now, slowly apply body weight to your top placement. Watch for shifting. If it seems fine under body weight, bounce lightly. Do not look up at the placement. If it pulls out, it could hit you in the eye. Once you are satisfied with this test, bounce severely on it. Use your body to gain dynamic up and down motion, thus increasing the weight being dynamically applied to your top piece.

Now that you have bounced on that top piece until you are blue in the face, move up onto it with full confidence and make your next placement. When you are doing your bounce test on the next placement, you will understand how nice it is to know that your previous one already held the test.

At first this "aggressive testing" seems nuts, but it enables you to link, with some degree of confidence, an incredible string of tricky and dubious aid placements.

SAFETY

There are several safety concerns when you are bounce testing. Wear a helmet. After pulling out a few dozen placements on my skull, I finally became tired of that routine. I wear a construction hard hat while aid climbing. The hard hat was such an enjoyable improvement that I wouldn't aid climb without one. The added feeling of safety allows me to climb better.

I also climb with a pair of clear safety glasses. One eye injury halfway up El Cap was enough. The tiny, flying metal fragments caused by pounding on pitons can end up in your eyes.

Think about what your hands, fingers and feet are doing. Fingers wrapped through the wrong carabiner could be easily broken during a fall. Be aware that if one of your feet is in the aider of your bottom piece, it will stay there if the top piece pulls out. It is possible that your stuck leg will take the force of the small fall before the bottom daisy chain catches you. This is another reason to be low while testing. Consider removing your foot from the bottom aider while testing the top piece. After a while, experience will help determine when it is safe to move fast or slowly. Move carefully. If your top piece suddenly pulls out, don't be discouraged. Try again and take enough time to do a better job.

There are certain placements that shouldn't be "bounce tested". Don't bounce test on hooks, the end sections of extremely expanding flakes, and body weight placements that obviously will not hold a bounce test. I have only seen a few of these.

Tricky aid placements are made easier by the psychological benefits of aggressive testing. One of the most enjoyable aspects of aid climbing is how you become totally engrossed in each placement. Sometimes it can take 30 minutes to arrange a placement. During that time you are totally engrossed and only occasionally become aware of your vulnerable and sometimes dangerous position.

Testing is the margin between the safe and insane.

ADVANCED AID PLACEMENTS

Testing the placements is fairly generic and mechanical. The fun part of the game is getting the tricky placements to stick. Advanced aid placements fall into the categories of hooking, expanding, heads, thin pins, and loose rock.

HOOKING Hooking seems tricky. Once a hook is passed, there usually is no protection. Be creative with hooks. It is possible to use hooks for protection by taping them in place with lots of duct tape. I have also found places where a downward hook can be tensioned against an upward hook for protection using an elastic bungee cord. More than a few times I have found hook placements that can be tapped with a hammer and seated over similar sized flakes. It is surprising how good these hammered-on hooks can be for aid and protection.

EXPANDING FLAKES A piece placed behind an expanding flake will expand the flake under body weight or expand it under the pressure of placing the piece. Although they sound scary, expanding flakes on the granite of El Capitan are not that hard to climb. Usually these flakes are so large and sound that they will expand to a certain point and stop. Hopefully, they won't break off. When climbing a long expanding section, try to make your first placement a piton that appears to be too big for the placement. If you can successfully hammer this one home, chances are the flake has expanded 70 percent of the distance it can go. This will help diminish the difficulties encountered for the remainder of the flake.

Try to alternate piton with nuts on an expanding flake. The first piton expands the flake 70 percent. The next placement is a nut that does not expand the flake. (a flake that is too small for camming devices). If this nut is put in a good slot, the third placement will be easy. The third placement might be a piton that continues to expand the flake. Be careful, as the flake expands, it tends to open up on your weighted piece. Too much and you will find yourself airborne. If you alternate the next placement with a piton, it expands the flake on your weighted piece, the nut. Since the nut is tapered, it will still hold in the placement. Now, as your piton expands the flake, try clipping your daisy chain into it. Even though you are still weighting the lower nut, the daisy will catch you if the piton expands the flake too far, causing the nut to pull out. Expanding flakes need to be expanded in order for their structure to have enough pressure to hold aid placements under bodyweight.

There are few hard and fast rules for expanding flakes. Be aware of the differences between expanding flake and loose flake. On a loose flake, the above method might be disastrous. Examine the every flake closely. Pound your hammer on the flake. This will yield an audible report of the flakes character. A deeper thud is better news than a higher pitched tin-like thud. A longer echo will indicate a more hollow flake.

Experiment with different gadgets for your placements. Remember, the flake should expand, but only in the right sequence. Slider nuts, Aliens, Tri-Cam Units, Quickies, and Ball Nuts are new tools that take the fright out of expanding flakes. Copperheads can be hammered into the right shape and used as nuts. Hooks can be useful for the edge of flakes. They act as a non-expanding placement between two expanding placements. Aggressive testing is not recommended; it may expand the flake more than body weight would.

COPPERHEADING Copperheads are the most common type of tricky aid placements. Those made from aluminum have greater sticking power for extreme placements. However, Alumniheads are only good for one placement. Heads are easy to place with the following rules. First find a depression, usually in the back of a corner, that will accept a head. Clean it out so the head will have a clean place to stick to. Scrape the depression with a thin piton or a putty knife. Hold the head in place and tap it with the tip of the hammer. Once the head is stationary, use a blunt chisel or steel punch to smash it into every conceivable atom of the rock. Hit it evenly so that it doesn't rock back and forth in the slot. Be careful not to cut the support cable with your hammer or chisel. Beat the head until completely satisfied, and then beat some more! Now use the aggressive test.

Placing heads doesn't get much more complicated than this. Sometimes you get involved in placing two or three heads near each other and using a tie off sling to equalize the weight. This is surprisingly effective for very marginal placements. Circleheads are aluminum or copperheads that are designed for horizontal placements. They act on similar principles as vertical copperheads. Copperheading is always an enjoyable part of aid climbing. It is fun for the leader, but not for the follower who must clean it using a jerking motion with the hammer.

THIN PITON PLACEMENTS Thin piton placements are the origin of tricky aid climbing. It is an aesthetic experience to drive knifeblade or Rurp pitons into a hairline, splitting crack on a bulging headwall on El Capitan. Remember, a piton that is too narrow for the crack may look great, but pull easily. A knifeblade driven perfectly into a shallow crack may hold bodyweight even though it goes in only 1/4 of an inch. Pins like these need to be tied off so they don't lever out. Tied off pins will be lost forever if they are pulled out, so consider putting a keeper sling through the eye and clipping that to your biner. A rurp has wonderful holding power but can be difficult to remove. Just recently a product called a Bird Beak is available for the thinnest seams. This ultra thin pin has a broader range of use than a Rurp, and it is much easier to remove. A Bird Beak works like a piton, but has a tomahawk shape that gives you some downward hooking action inside the crack. This little pin is also bent at the shaft so that you get some sideways torque at the same time. Tony Yaniro had something similar to a Bird Beak in the late 1970's and he called it a Star. The biggest caution for placing thin pins is in bottoming cracks. Over driving can cause the pins to bottom out and loosen. Aggressive testing is highly recommended for thin pins.

Figure 7-1
Placing a copperhead.

LOOSE ROCK Loose rock is what will scare most aid climbers to the bone. No route is worth dying for. Be cautious as you nail your way around car-sized loose blocks. The best way to climb loose blocks is to first analyze how they are attached. Take your time to check for visual fracture points and lightly tap on the block in various places with your hammer to determine points of strength and weakness. Look for dirt between the block or flake and the main wall. Dirt makes a poor mortar. This means be careful. Next check for possible ways to avoid the block by aid climbing in a different direction. If you must climb the block, think about free climbing since this puts much less direct pressure on any single point. Aid climb with caution and try to avoid hammering pins behind the block. Don't use the bounce test on loose blocks. Finally, analyze what will happen to you and your rope if the block comes off. Try to route your rope in a safe direction, or use two ropes. Kiss your helmet and wish for the best.

It is impossible to categorize every different type of tricky aid placement that you might encounter. Rather, it is better advice to climb systematically and thus save yourself the mental and physical energy by safely engineering each difficult placement to perfection. Use efficiency to gain speed in aid climbing. Don't be careless in order to go fast. One 150 foot fall could zipper out 6 hours of hard work and land you on a granite ledge. Rationalize each tricky placement and bounce test whenever safely possible This way you can string together a pitch of A4 or A5 and feel reasonably good about it. Bring all of the comforts of home and stay motivated. Enjoy the exposure, and if you happen to drop a piton, take a minute to watch it fall from your grasp and accelerate through the hot summer air. As it gains speed, it will tumble and then violently slice through the air. A peregrine falcon may even be fooled for a second and dive after it. Enjoy the show, enjoy the exposure, and don't forget to solve that puzzle in front of you, that tricky aid placement. It is but one in a thousand on your way to the top.

8. CLIMBING BIG WALLS FAST

By Steve Schnieder

Climbing big walls fast is for anyone who loathes the act of hauling bags, or simply does not want to miss a single night in the Yosemite Lodge bar. Imagine climbing El Cap with just a light rack and a daypack with a few munchies. You and your partner move well together at a rate of 200/300 feet per hour. Halfway through the day, the summit is 1000 feet away. The absence of the haul bag gives the ascent an aura of commitment. On the next ledge, you pass another party on the third day of their climb. A few hours later, you summit out on top. Hurry down, and take a shower before treating yourself to a meal in the restaurant. This sounds great and it is. For those willing to free themselves of a haul bag's security and accompanying slowness, speed climbing big walls is the game to play.

HISTORY

The whole speed climbing game really started with Jim Bridwell, Billy Westbay, and John Long's 1975 one day ascent of the Nose in fifteen hours. This historic ascent is more astounding because the trio used only pitons, and had to nail up every aid section of the climb. It was a major breakthrough in the way big walls were approached at the time. For most parties El Cap is a multi-day outing requiring numerous nights and grueling hauling. In one day, El Cap became like a backyard crag. As the years went by, the Nose received several one day ascents. Each ascent decreased the time spent on the wall. One of the best speed climbers in the world, Hans Florin, and I climbed the nose in 8 hours and 2 minutes.

Speed ascents have been made on other routes as well. Rick Cashner and Mike Corbett teamed up again and again to make one day ascents of the West Buttress and Lurking Fear on El Cap, the Direct NW Face of Half Dome, and the Harding route on Mt. Watkins. Exactly ten years after the first one day ascent of the Nose, John Bachar and Peter Croft climbed the Nose and the Regular NW Face of Half Dome in a single day. Climbers are really cruising some routes quickly.

How do these climbers go so fast? Well, they didn't just jump on El Cap first thing. Shorter walls such as Middle Cathedral and the Washington Column are good training routes for El Cap. It's a natural progression to go from a one day ascent of the Column to either the West Face of El Cap or the Regular Route on Half Dome. If a party can pull in a time of 8 to 9 hours on the Column, they should be able to do Half Dome in 15 to 17 hours.

Learn to estimate how long a route will take by looking at the topo. For a well rounded climbing team, 5.9/5.10 pitches should take around 30/40 minutes to lead and clean. It is good practice to write down an optimistic time schedule for the climb. Afterwards, see how well you did. It will give you a good understanding of your abilities and limits.

RULES
There are not any rules for speed climbing. Pulling on pieces, standing on bolts or shoulders is considered legit. Don't get caught up in trying to free climb a hard pitch, because it's slower and less efficient than just aiding the pitch. Remember, the goal is to make last call in the Mountain Room bar at the Lodge. Fixing pitches is considered taboo. A climb is not truly done in one day if fixed ropes have been used.

BETA
There are a lot ways to help speed things up on a big wall. The best tip is to eliminate the haul bag. The second climber can carry a daypack containing all the necessary supplies for a one day ascent. Also, know your route. If neither member of the team has done the route before, ask someone who has and get the lowdown on the climb. Some pitches may be combined into one. Running two pitches together can cut down on time spent at belays. Determine the rack for each pitch. Dragging along the wide stuff on a finger crack is a waste of energy. Identify tricky places where it is possible to get lost. A party can't make a fast time if they are doddling along off route. There may be extra water on the route. Sometimes gallons of water will be left on bivouac ledges as prior parties seek to trim their loads.

DRAFT THEORY
The second climber can either free climb or jumar the pitch. Jumaring is

generally faster, except maybe on traverses. On really fast climbs, one must "hit" the jugs like they are jogging up a hill. A straightforward pitch can be jumared in two or three minutes. However, be careful that the jumars are biting and make sure you are tied in.

It is also good strategy to have one person lead a block of five or six pitches in a row. The leader gets a rest while the partner jumars up, instead of the tired partner leading the next pitch. The designated leader is ready to fire off the pitch faster than his tired partner could have done.

The leader has the pressure of keeping the momentum going. Conversely, the man jumaring is in the sub-role. Jumaring takes little mental effort. I call this the drafting technique, since it is similar to a bike racer drafting off the leader of a pack. After five or six pitches, the second climber is ready to take his duties out on the sharp end of the rope.

BELAYS

Simple belays are mandatory for a fast climb. If there are decent slings at the anchor, the leader should clip in with two opposing carabiners and tie in with a figure eight knot. Otherwise, tie off the best two pieces with clove hitches and yell down to your partner to hit it. The second then races up the rope. Instead of tying in to the rope, each climber is clipped into the end of the rope with two opposing carabiners. When the second arrives at the belay, he clips in with a quick draw composed of locking biners. The two climbers then switch ends of the rope. The second gives the rack to the leader and he is off.

A quick rhythm through each belay can make a climb go faster. It should only take a minute or two. Remember, any task that is done once on every pitch, is repeated 35 times on the Nose's 35 pitches. Five minutes at each belay on the Nose is three hours spent at belays on the entire route. A team should try to operate like a well-oiled machine. Wall slick and well tuned.

FOOD AND WATER

The right amount of food, water and gear is a key to success. Going light as possible is essential. When Rick Cashner and I made the first one day ascent of the Salathe in 14 hours, all we had were two bananas, two Baby Ruth bars, two quarts of water, and two sweaters in a small daypack that the second jumared with. We walked down in climbing shoes. Some more water and food would have been nice, but our commitment to making the climb in one day helped us go faster. Now, I'm a little smarter. I bring a bunch of Power Bars and a couple of apples or oranges. Power Bars have a high energy- to-weight ratio, and eliminate the ups and downs of sugar rushes that come from eating candy bars. Water can also be laced with an energy supplement. It is hard to carry enough water to be fully comfortable on a big wall speed climb. You will likely become dehydrated and use up your body's reserves. Try to get by on a quart or two per person for a full day. If possible, plan your climb to maximize climbing in the shade. This will help cut down on water use.

BE PREPARED

While leading the thirtieth pitch of Salathe, the Roof, a piece I was standing on popped, sending me for a short ride into space. On the way down I broke my two front teeth, and opened up a gash in my index finger. Dangling in midair, slightly concussed, the gravity of our situation became all too real. It was 2500' feet down to the ground, and 500 hundred feet up to the rim, only a couple of hours of light left, and no bivy gear. We were pushing the edge a bit. I managed to finish the pitch, and Rick led uneventfully to the summit.

A first aid kit should be taken for bandaging wounds sustained en route. At least bring some adhesive tape. A second rope, lightweight 7-9mm thick, should be carried in a pack or trailed in case circumstances dictate a retreat. Most trade routes on El Cap such as the Nose, Salathe` and the West Face can be rappelled fairly quickly because of the abundance of fixed anchors. If daytime is running out too fast, a quick retreat can replace a miserable bivy. It is irresponsible to go on a big wall without a second rope.

SIMUL-CLIMBING

Climbing simultaneously with your partner can save valuable time in places, but is very dangerous. On easier ground, when the leader runs out the rope, the belayer removes his anchor, and both climbers ascend the rock, separated by a ropelength. The leader continues to put in protection, so there is always three or four protection pieces between the climbers. It is a bad idea for anyone to fall while simul-climbing. But, it is worse if the bottom person falls, because he will jerk the leader off his holds. If the leader falls, it is not as bad as the bottom climber holds only a normal leader fall. The stronger climber in the team should be on the bottom in simul-climbing situations. Vogler and Critchelow used simul-climbing techniques on their record Nose time. Bachar and Croft also simul-climbed much of Half Dome in their record double ascent of Half Dome and El Cap.

Personally, I only like to simul-climb with someone whose climbing abilities I trust. Even then, I don't go over 5.7/5.8. On harder pitches, I like the rest one gets with having the second jumar. Also, it is a lot easier to jug 5.10 than it is to climb 5.10. On my recent record ascent of El Cap, we did not simul-climb. At the speed we were climbing, it was too dangerous.

Simul-climbing can also be used to run two pitches together. If a full ropelength will put the leader within twenty feet of a belay while running two pitches together, the last twenty feet can be simul-climbed. The second climber can undo his anchor and climb twenty feet higher, so the leader can make the higher belay. The skipped belay saves time.

A longer rope can be even more useful in these situations. A 175' or 180' rope often help run two pitches together. It works great on the Nose. A lightweight leadline of 10.5 or 10mm is optimal for trimming a couple of extra pounds.

BIG WALL NAIL UPS

Up until 1989, nobody had ever done a real nailing route on El Cap in a 24 hour time period, as speed climbing "days" are called. John Middendorf and Mike Corbett came close on The Shield. Arriving on Chickenhead Ledge, with just a few pitches to go and ample time to finish the route, headlamp problems forced them to halt their climb until morning. They missed a sweet victory by hours.

While it is relatively easy to cruise fast on big walls that are predominantly free routes, it is much harder to go fast on nailing routes. The process of banging in a pin every five feet can slow most parties to a snail's pace. During the full moon in April 1989, Rick Cashner, Werner Braun, and Kevin Fosberb made a stunning nineteen hour ascent of the Zodiac on El Cap. They used some special tricks to shave hours off their time down. Climbing with three people is optimal for pure speed. There are more people to divide the work of nailing umpteen pitches in a row. On the Zodiac, Werner and Kevin did all the leading on the route, while Rick cleaned every pitch. Each climber had a specialized task to do, with time for some rest in between. The trio also carried two racks with them. As soon as a pitch was led, the other leader would jug up with the second rack and begin leading the next pitch, while leaving Rick to clean the pitch. There was always someone leading. A smart tactic.

They started at 12:20 AM and finished at 7:20 PM. This timing meant that they got their night climbing out of the way at the start while they were fresh. In the last pitches to the rim, when they were the most tired, they were able to use the final hours of sunlight to help them along.

TIMING - WHEN TO BLAST

The time of day chosen to start a big wall speed climb is very important. It can mean the difference between success or failure. For a route taking twelve hours, simply start at first light and climb all day long. For a route taking 15 or 16 hours, takeoff time should be about one or two in the morning, planning to top out in the sun's last rays. For a project that might take a full 24 hours blast-off at six or seven in the evening. Try to get a fast start in the last light of the day to establish good momentum. Night climbing is easier to deal with in a fresh state. Night climbing at the end of a grueling day can be mentally demoralizing and should be avoided. Try to maintain a steady pace throughout the night. A couple of short breaks will help maintain freshness. Be extra careful at night and don't rush things, just go steady.

When dawn hits the wall, a party should be halfway up their intended route. Since not as much water is needed during night, water is conserved. The top half of the wall is often cooler than the lower half because of breeze and elevation. Near the top, the stronger climber should take the lead, and fire off the anchor leg to the summit. June is the best month, with daylight in Yosemite lasting until nine in the evening. If the ascent takes a little over 24 hours, a party starting at 6:00 PM the previous day can use these last few hours to top out without resorting to anymore night climbing. A pack of matches or a lighter is wise to have in case a party tops out, but is too tired to hike down. A comfortable bivy can be improvised around a hot fire. For those strong enough to hike down the same day or night, they should not attempt to drive their car for any length of time. The amount of fatigue is awesome. One can feel great about the climb, but be ready to pass out in the next second. Be aware, especially if you are faced with a descent.

CLIMBING AT NIGHT

Climbing at night is an unnatural experience. The walls become silent as the swallows settle in. A climber's attention becomes focused on a few square meters illuminated by a headlamp. Night climbing is where big wall speed climbs are won or lost. To make things easier, it is always good to plan a route on the full moon. Although a headlamp is still needed for placing protection and climbing, the extra light can help make route finding easier. Ropes are visible as they hang below, and can be flipped out of cracks that might not be seen on a dark night. The second pitch of the Salathe, and the Stovelegs on the Nose are hot spots for getting ropes stuck.

A party should always carry a complete extra headlamp, and not just an extra battery. If a headlamp is lost in a fall what good would an extra battery be? Petzl headlamps seem to be the most comfortable and have a zoom lens that can be adjusted. Avoid the type of headlamp that has a wire leading to a battery pack worn on the hip or carried in a pocket. The wire gets in the way while climbing. Self contained headlamps are the easiest to use.

Climbing at night takes experience, and should be practiced before attempting a speed ascent. Once the skill is mastered, it should take about the same time to lead a pitch day or nigh. Personally, I like to take it a bit slower while climbing at night. Mistakes can happen easier in the shadows of the night. Once while following a set of pendulums at night, I was shocked to realize I was only clipped in to one of my jumars. It was the type of stupid life threatening mistake that is harder to make in the light of the day. Be wary!

PASSING PARTIES

Encountering a slower party brings up a delicate problem. How to pass? First try explaining that they are slowing down your party. Explain that you have no bivy gear. My best line is that I am trying to make a date in the bar that very night. This works most of the time.

In other situations, like when foreigners can't understand you, or when you run into a party that feels you have no right to pass them on their wall, it is time to get rude. Just because someone is leading a pitch doesn't mean there isn't room for another leader. Clip into their belay so they can't undo their anchors and start climbing. Clip their protection pieces en route. When their leader makes a belay, make yours five feet higher. They will realize that, yes, you are passing and they might as well comply. This is serious. Don't spend a miserable night on the wall just to be polite.

ED. NOTE - This method of passing is rude. It can result in nasty consequences. A party passed another party on Middle Cathedral Rock, despite protestations. The first party said they feared climbers on the loose rock above. The second party dislodged a rock, severely injuring a member of the first party. A law suit resulted. Although loose rock is always a danger and a helmet should have been worn, passing parties is a delicate situation. Be careful how you treat others and their equipment, and do not do anything that jeopardizes anothers' safety.

The world of big-wall speed-climbing is available to anyone in reasonable shape and totally psyched for a particular ascent. Working up a ladder with short walls on the bottom and big walls on the top is the basic training technique. The big prize in Yosemite is the Nose-in-a-day. It might seem impossible at first. Attitude and motivation are the biggest factors in speed climbing. The Nose has even been done in one day on-sight by a party that was simply talked into doing it by friends. Rick Cashner once described the joy he takes in speed climbing. "There's nothing like being on the ground, and looking up at a big wall that you've already climbed that day." That's when you really deserve a brewski.

9. CLIMBING SOLO ON BIG WALLS

By Steve Schnieder

It is one thing to climb a big wall with a partner, and it is altogeter another thing to solo a big wall, The task of leading, rappelling, cleaning, and hauling each pitch combine to make soloing a big wall about three times as much effort as with a partner. There aren't any reprieves like when a partner is taking four hours to lead a pitch, and the best thing for the belayer to do is to read a couple of chapters in a favorite spy novel. The idea of a rest while soloing sounds good, it but negates any upward progress.

Conversely, a soloist is never bored with himself on a big wall because there is simply too much work to be done. Soloing a big wall takes a resoluteness of character. It is not an undertaking for the wishy-washy. The rewards are outstanding. For those who have summited a Grade V or VI, they know what I mean. Having climbed every inch by themselves, relying on no one else, the feelings of self-reliance and accomplishment are boundless.

SOLO HISTORY

Royal Robbins got big wall soloing off the ground with his ascent of the Leaning Tower in 1963. Five years later, an inspired Robbins made a daring solo ascent, second overall, of the Muir Wall on El Capitan. The effort took nine grueling days. Around this time, Eric Beck completed the first solo of Half Dome. Now that the biggest faces had been soloed, the next step was to solo a first ascent on the big stone. This prize went to Jim Dunn, who soloed Cosmos in 1972. The same year saw Charlie Porter solo two new routes on El Cap.

What now remained was for a person to solo an extremely hard aid line on El Cap. Rob Slater did this with his solo of the Pacific Ocean wall in the early 1980's. Once hailed as the hardest aid climb in the world, his fast time of five days makes his ascent additionally impressive. The next stunner was Duane Raleigh's ascent of Zenyatta Mendatta in the mid 1980's. Along with the Sea of Dreams, this was the most difficult line on El Cap, with many A5 pitches. Charles Cole made the most difficult solo first ascent when he climbed Space on El Cap. He also pioneered a difficult new line on Half Dome, Queen of Spades, earning himself a niche in Yosemite history. As the 80's continued, many other lines fell to solo climbers. Randy Leavitt, Steve Grossman, and Walt Shipley were also impressive solo climbers of this era. Xavier Bongard, a Swiss climber, amazed the locals with his solos of Jolly Rodger and Lost in America, both rated A5. But these ascents were eclipsed by his most recent solo of the Sea of Dreams. Once thought impossible to solo-the Sea of Dreams is the hardest aid route ever soloed.

SOLO SYSTEMS

If the aspiring climber chooses to solo big walls, he will need a rope solo system. Ten years ago, the only published method was the Barnett system, featured in Royal Robbins' minibook Advanced Rockcraft. The essence of the Barnett system is a "super" prusik loop that cinches the leadline in a leader fall. My friend, Rob Settlemire, used this system while soloing the Leaning Tower, his first big wall climb ever. He took one fall. The prusik failed to properly cinch up and started to burn through. As he accelerated toward ground zero he was fortunately stopped after 25' by a backup knot he had tied in earlier. This story illustrates two points. One, that the Barnett system was basically useless and that another system needed to be invented. Two, the backup knot that Rob tied saved his life, and should be an integral item in any solo system.

For the would be soloist of the nineties, technology has caught up with the modern era. Hard routes on El Cap, including new routes, have been done solo using a variety of rope solo methods. Each person must decide which system is best for himself.

Keep in mind that solo leader fall will result in an upward pull on the anchors (once the soloist has clipped in his first protection piece). All systems discussed assume that the anchor have a directional anchor for an upward pull.

FIVE SOLOING METHODS

1) **TYING KNOTS** This system is the simplest. Anchor the rope solidly. Once the anchor is clipped into, simply grab up ten or 15 feet of slack, tie a figure eight knot, and clip in with two opposing carabiners. The soloist is now solidly tied into the rope. Place protection and clip in the rope as normal. When the ten or fifteen feet of slack runs out, simply tie another knot down the rope with the desired length and clip into another set of opposing carabiners. Now unclip

and untie the previous knot, and slack will be obtained for the next section of rock.

The advantage of this system is its simplicity and security. No costly gadgets are required so it is economical. However, this system is cluttered with ropes and knots hanging everywhere. Unless one is a magician, this system will require two hands to tie and untie the knots, severely limiting one's ability to free climb.

Figure 9-1
Clove hitch.

2) **CLOVE HITCH METHOD** This system is the same as above except that a cinched clove hitch is used with the two opposing carabiners instead of a figure eight. When slack is needed, the clove hitch can be lossened up and rope fed through as desired, then cinched tight again. The clove hitch acts as a "running knot", avoiding the constant tying and untying as in the preveous method. Two hands are required to feed the rope through. While not good for free climbing, this system is secure for aid climbing, and has been the method of choice for many hard solo ascents on El Cap. Again, this method is as economical as can be.

3) **THE CHARLES COLE METHOD** This system was devised around 1986 by Charles Cole for free climbing while roped soloing. The rope is anchored in. A bight or loop of rope is made next to the anchor and passed through a belay plate, and clipped into two opposing carabiners on the harness. To the rope trailing downward, not the anchor end, attach a jumar in the upright position. The jumar is clipped into the side of the harness with a three feet sling. The idea is this: in the event of a fall, the jumar will act as a hand by the belay plate as in a regular belay. One climbs and protects as normal. When slack is needed, press the trigger on the jumar and pull the jumar sideways. If more than a couple of feet is needed, grab the rope between the belay plate and jumar with the teeth, assuming the other hand is holding onto the rock, then release the trigger and pull for more slack. Repeating the process until the desired slack is released.

This solo system is tricky and requires at least a few hours of practice to master. It does allow the climber to venture out of his aiders and free climb easier sections of rock. However, the act of constantly pulling a jumar for slack is tiring, and thus only moderate freeclimbing (5.10 and below) seems reasonable. Harder than 5.10, it is probably easier to aid climb the route using this system. This system makes for faster climbing than methods 1 and 2, since it feeds easier.

Although Charles Cole has fallen while using this system on El Cap, a large fall would not be recommended. The cam on the jumar is holding most the force of the fall. Test conducteed by John Dill, head of Yosemite Valley Search and Rescue , show that jumar cams start cutting into ropes at around a force of 1000 pounds. Since 2000 pound forces can be generated in the largest leader falls, this is something to think about seriously. Also, remember that jumars are weak and can break. Such falls may break the jumar.

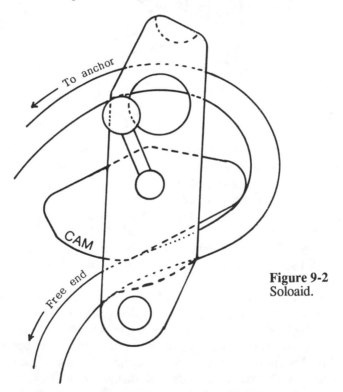

Figure 9-2
Soloaid.

4) THE SOLOIST AND SOLOAID These two items, made by Rock Exoctica are mechanical solo devices. The Soloist is the free climbing version, while the Soloaid is more suited to big wall aid climbs. Both devices have a special cam that locks the rope in place in the event of a fall. The Soloist feeds the rope well, so the climber is able to free climb near his normal limit. The Soloist works on a directional, however, and the cam does not engage in an upside-down fall. This is dicey, to say the least. Another drawback is that as one nears the top of a lead, the weight of the rope tends to pull the rope through the device, causing slack at the belay. Also, a chest harness is needed with both these devices. For these reasons it is hard to recommend the Soloist.

The Soloaid is stronger than the Soloist - it has an extra gizmo that makes it safe in upside down falls. It requires one hand to feed the rope, but is an improvement over the clove hitch system. Free climbing is limited to easier ground due to the one-handed feeding process, but the device works quite well for pure aid climbing. The Soloist and Soloaid are a little expensive, but so are all the accoutrements required to make up a big wall ensemble.

5) THE SILENT PARTNER In this case, I've saved the best for last. The Silent Partner is the coup-de-grace of solo devices. The Silent Partner was invented by Mark Blanchard of Mammoth Lakes, California. Having soloed several big wall in the Valley, Blanchard developed this device through trial and error over several years, with the result being a state-of-the-art product for the 90's.

The Silent Partner looks like a beefed up pulley. The heart of this "pulley" is the drum which encases a speed activated mechanism that locks up when spun fast, similiar to a seat belt. A clove hitch is tied around the drum and the device clipped into the climber's sit harness. In a fall, the drum locks up and the clove hitch cinches the rope.

The rope feeds well through the Silent Partner, and it always holds a climber's fall - upside down, sideways, and head over heels.

Methods 3 and 4 employ a cam that effectively pinch the rope in a fall, the result can be tough on the rope. The clove hitch of the Silent Partner is easy on the rope in a fall. It works equally well for free climbing and aid climbing, and is simply the best gadget going. The Silent Partner is again a spendy item, costing a little more than the Soloist, but worth every penny when your life is on the line.

WARNING - All these devices should be used with backup knots placed every once-in-a-while, at the leader's discretion, and tied into the end of the rope.

Enough said about solo devices, it's time to get down to the tricks of the trade. Getting the beta on the gear needed on each pitch is especially critical in solo climbing. If the solo climber doesn't know what kind of rack to take for a pacticular pitch, take everything, since he cannot call for extra gear in the middle of a pitch as with a partner.

ROPEWORK

The solo climber is entirely responsible for the ropes. Special care must be taken to ensure that the ropes feed well throughout the entire pitch. With loops of the leadline hanging because of backup knots, keeping the rope out of cracks where it could get stuck is a constant job. Strong winds can send the rope side-

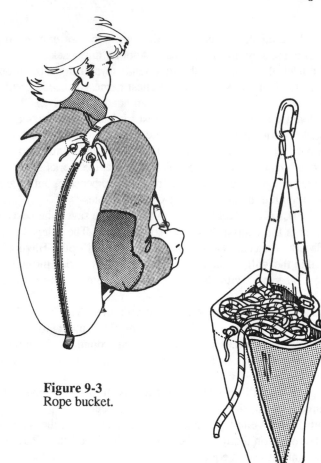

Figure 9-3
Rope bucket.

ways onto "keeper" flakes. In these situations, a "ropebucket", such as the one made by A5 Adventures, can be helpful. Placing the end of the leadline in the bucket at the belay will allow for a feeding system to help keep the rope off snags. Lacking a bucket, the rope can actually be carried by the soloist on the lead. The hauline can be stacked in the top of the haulbag so it is also safe from snags.

On my first attempt to solo the Nose in one day, I made a mistake while leading Boot Flake. I had inadvertently tied both ends of my leadline into the anchors, I came to the middle of the rope, 20 feet from the top of the "Boot", before I realized I had both ends tied in and I was stuck. I constructed an anchor with my five remaining friends - 3 for a downward pull and 2 for an upward pull - in the expanding Boot Flake, and rappelled back down. I split this pitch in two and lost about 20-30 minutes of valuable time. I resolved to get my act together, forget about the time I had lost, and continue without mishap.

RAPPELLING AND HAULING PITCHES

Once the pitch is led, it must be rapelled, cleaned, and hauled. Rappelling traversing pitches requires special care. When there is a lot of slack between belays as on short pitches, rappel down until the rope goes tight, and then jumar across. Clip into the rope with a sling and carabiners to backup the jumars. On long traversing pitches, it is nice to have two trail lines. One rope is clipped into the anchor and the other is not. When the traverse is completed, one can rappel the freehanging trail line down, and then jumar up to the anchor via the other trail line. Be sure to remember to bring the jumars on the lead.

Once at the belay after rappelling, the haul bag must be lifted off the belay, and left to hang by the haul line anchored above. An easy way to do this is to use a third jumar to gain slack in the haul line. The jumar is clipped into the haul line with a sling attached directly from the jumar to the haul bag. The rope is then pulled down with one hand at the same time the jumar is pushed up with the other hand. When the jumar grips, the rope stretch helps pull the bag up, allowing the climber to unclip from the anchor and send it on its way. Lower the haul bag out, if it is going to smash the rock in a free swing. Set up the hauling system before rappelling with a combination jumar/pulley devilce. Otherwise, when one reaches the belay after cleaning a pitch, he is faced with the problem of getting a tensioned rope through a pulley to set up the hauling system.

CLEANING PITCHES

Now it's time to clean the pitch. The leadline must be pulled down until all slack is removed in the system before moving onto the rope with jumars. While soloing the Rostum's last pitch, Mark Blanchard thought hc had pulled all the slack down. He had jumared to the lip of the roof, when- WHOOOOOOSH-he felt himself falling through the air. Unknowingly, there had been almost 40 feet of slack on top. The rope had wedged in a carabiner near the top, holding his weight, only to peel as Mark rounded the roof. Miraculously, Mark only went 20 feet before the rope snagged again in another carabiner, with 20 feet of slack left to pop at any moment. Totally shaken up, Mark made the most gingerly jumar of his life back to the top. The lesson is this - The solo climber must make sure the leadline will not hang up while he is rappelling down the haul line. This may involve pulling the leadline down through the protection pieces as he descends the pitch.

Cleaning the pitch is exactly the same as with a partner. When reaching the belay, the haulbag must be hauled. Getting a haulbag stuck while soloing is a real bummer. There isn't a second person along to free the bag. The soloist could rappell down to the stuck bag, free it, and jumar back up, only to have the bag get stuck five feet higher. This is not exactly a picnic in the park. If the bag gets stuck within 80 feet of the belay, the soloist should use the dead weight method. Rappells the leadline down next to the bag, and clips onto the haul line to haul as normal. Manually extract the bag from where it's stuck and keep the bag free the rest of the way.

Figure 9-4
Solo space haul system.
Note: Haul bag on a fifi can be
dangerous.

If the bag is stuck more than 80 feet down, and looks like it will get stuck again and again, this system can still be used, but will require a third rope. Simply tie the third rope into the end of the hauline to extend it. Rappel the leadline to the bag, and haul as normal on the third rope.

SPEED SOLOING

This game combines the quickness of speed ascents with the self reliance and perserverance of soloing. Jim Beyer ushered in this new era with his 1987 landmark one day solo of El Cap via the West Face in 23.5hrs. In 1989, I bagged two great prizes-The first one day solo ascent of the Nose of El Cap in 21:22 and the first one day solo of Half Dome via the Direct Northwest Face in 21:58 hrs. A list of speed climbs with partners is a prerequisite to these endeavors.

Speed soloing big wall is an unimaginable test of physical strength and mental endurance. One is pushed way beyond normal limits. The speed soloer must carry all his own food and water - a severe handicap. It would be nice to have a couple of gallons of water to drink during such a formidable task, but the weight of two gallons <16 pounds> is too much to start out a climb with. The speed soloer should travel light from the start and just plan on getting fully wasted by the end of the climb.

When I speed soloed Half Dome, I made my ascent in October when temperatures were cooler. I took only three quarts of water, hoping to find some leftover water along the way. I found none. Though I became very dehydrated, I had a supply of 7 or 8 Power bars to munch along the way. The simple and complex carbohydrates found in Power bars provided a platform of sustained energy that propelled me to the top. I had done the route ten years before, and remembered that no pitons were needed past Grand Terrace, the halfway point. I lightened my load a few pounds by throwing my pin rack off in a stuffsack with an orange streamer tape attached for easy retrieval. I recovered my pins on the hike back down. (ED. Note: This practice is not recommended for El Capitan or any cliff that may have people at it's base)

Another stunt I pulled was to free solo the Crescent Crack, a deep 5.5 chimney. I left my daypack and rack at the belay on a Fifi Hook. This way I could pull my pack up and save the work of rapelling and jumaring an awkward chimney pitch. I did run the risk of the fifi hook somehow coming off and sending the pack hurtling to the ground. As the rope came tight, there would've been a helluva downward jerk on myself while free soloing. These tricks saved me a lot of work and precious time, and are an example of how to adapt strategy to a particular route.

LAST TIPS

Remember, soloing a big wall is a hearty undertaking. The retreat rate is high for solo attempts. Don't be discouraged if minor mishaps occur. Try to take them in stride. Be equipped to retreat. If the need arises for a rescue, try to effect a self rescue. When a soloist gets rescued, it makes all soloing look dicey.

For the successful big wall soloist, there are many personal rewards. Expect to be damn proud of a job well done.

10. FIRST ASCENTS

By Steve Grossman

It seems inevitable to be struck with curiosity about the first ascent while climbing an established big wall. What were the original cracks like? What sort of hardware did the first climbers have? Were there any storms or big peels? Early routes on El Capitan set high standards for commitment and style. These routes were done with a rack of pitons, the bare minimum of food and water, and a few bolts. The written accounts are adventure classics. Yvon Chouinard and T.M. Herbert's ascent of the Muir Wall is one of the finest examples of boldness and commitment. After three thousand feet of climbing, they were left with one bolt and one quart of water.

Even today, with the most sophisticated gear and techniques, several thousand feet of unclimbed stone pose a formidable problem. If the puzzle is solved creatively, using commitment backed up by solid technique, then the resulting experience can be among the most satisfying and rewarding that climbing has to offer.

Once you have repeated several exisisting big wall routes, then the desire to stray off the beaten path may take hold of you. Before you try something different and new, try climbing some of the harder big walls. Develop the skills and the psyche necessary to push your limits on difficult, new ground. Be comfortable. And committed.

The coveted line may be among the first on a backcountry wall or a line between established routes on a frequented cliff. Wilderness areas have the most extensive potential for new routes. They offer the fullest sense of adventure enriched by the beauty and remoteness of the setting. Far from easy rescue and crowds, the emphasis is more on safety and exploration then on difficulty.

More developed areas have less to offer the aspiring first ascensionist. New routes tend to require considerably more work piecing together sinuous incipient features that have been overlooked. Thus, the walls tend to be more difficult and require the ability to climb at the hardest standards to prevent excessive and often unnecessary drilling.

Conflicts may arise from the local climbing community. Pressure to climb in good style and according to local precedent, can be intense. A perceived lack of ability or judgement can detract from the satisfaction of completing a first ascent. Such is the case with Wings of Steel on El Capitan. The first ascent party ignored local ethics and bolted excessively. The climbing community retaliated, ostracizing the climbers from the Valley forever.

With unclimbed rock at a premium, such pressures prompt those considering a new route to reflect seriously on their skill level before attempting a new route in a developed area. It is sad to see a potentially fine route brashly botched up. Easy access, rapid rescue and the security of watchful eyes below create an environment that is conducive to pushing one's technical and psychological limits; however, it may be best to seek first ascents in a place where help is miles away, and thoughtful, courageous climbing is required. In this way, you avoid the scorn of others and revel in the boldness of your own achievements.

Having arrived upon a route possibility, it is worth asking yourself a few hard questions. The response can serve to place the route in perspective and provide a framework to prepare for it logistically.

First, where will the route go? Careful examination of the cracks and other features that the route may follow is essential to choosing the best line. Creative route-finding will ideally select the most aesthetically pleasing sections of the wall. Link them together avoiding loose rock and blank stretches that may require bolting. The most appealing option may not be the easiest. Weigh the considerations such as speed, difficulty, weather and number of bolts required. First ascents are far more complicated than repeats. Your decisions will affect everyone's experience on the route in the future.

A detailed map of the route, constructed at the base by careful observation, can be very useful as you work from feature to feature. It is unwise to rely on memory alone. Visibility is often restricted while leading. Good cracks and other landmarks can be quite close and yet be unrecognizable.

Binoculars and high powered spotting scopes are commonly used to investigate crack sizes and bivy sites. Watch the shadows as they migrate across the wall during the day; a long shadow indicates a prominent feature. Snow deposition tells where you might find ledges. Water stains indicate where water flows and cracks may appear. But be careful. Do not mistake a water stain for a crack. The unfortunate result will be an unexpected bolt ladder. Be şure your route is a route, before you get up there.

Once you are assured the route will go, draw a map of the proposed line and use it to help prepare for the ascent. Get a rough idea of the sizes and quantity of hardware needed, the number of climbing days necessary (which determines how much food and water you'll need), and the number of bolts needed and their probable locations. A map aids in logistical planning as well as vertical navigation.

The next question is: Can we complete the route safely? In addition to climbing ability, safety requires that adequate precautions are taken, This includes foul weather gear, a first aid kit, and enough supplies to handle any eventualities. Self-sufficiency is a must. Losing a crucial piece of equipment or a small cut that gets infected, could lead to serious consequences. Be sure you are prepared and have alternate plans in case of mishap.

But how does one climb a route safely, without compromising style? Questions of safety and style depend on the experience of the climber and the difficulties they encounter. An inexperienced climber may place a bolt where a marginal piton placement might go. Also, the psychological and physical strain of route finding, placements, hauling and the ever present weight of the unknown, may force a climber to make decisions he'll regret later. Bear this in mind: it is worth picking a line that is well within your ability for your first new route. You can adjust to the slower pace and greater exertion involved. Really concentrate on each placement. Resorting to extensive drilling or bashing to overcome difficulty diminishes the subsequent climbing experience for everyone. Greater experience and finesse allows a less destructive approach to the first ascent.

It deserves mention that two distinct styles exist when placements run out and drilling becomes necessary. The traditional method assumes that the challenge in aid climbing lies in placements that are re-usable. Drilled placements should be a rivet or a bolt capable of holding more than body weight. The opposing style, the New Wave, assume that the technical and psychological challenge should be maximized. Drilled placements need only be sufficient to hold body weight and not capable of holding a fall. This ethic allows drilling of holes for hooks, enhancing natural hook placements and chiseling or drilling trenches for copperheads where no usable placements exist.

While the longer run outs and greater fall potential add to the challenge left for the next party, it is debatable whether risking lengthy falls is worth it, when the technical challenge has already been reduced.

Imagine that you are faced with two thirty foot corners separated by a blank section. In the corners are body weight copperhead placements. The traditional approach would allow for a bolt between the two corners to reduce the length of the fall. The new wave approach calls for hook holes between the two corners. The traditional climber would risk a sixty foot maximum fall; the new wave climber would risk a hundred foot fall. However, once the new wave climber reaches the second corner, they will continue to enhance the placements, to be sure that a fall will not take place. By upping the risk, they have reduced challenge.

Likewise, the New Wave approach legitimates use of drill and chisel on subsequent ascents. If a climber can bring the rock down to his level, then the next party has every right to do so as well. The traditional approach assumes that all drilled placements are fixed, and obligates the next party to use conventional gear. This serves to maintain the technical challenge for subsequent parties. The two approaches conflict when a New Wave climber ascends a bold traditional route. If a leader cannot differentiate between the two styles, he or she may reach for the chisel when things get dicey. Unknowing, they have diminished the stylistic and technical challenge left by previous ascent parties.

A good example of this is the Jolly Roger route on El Capitan. When first climbed this route had some of the most difficult natural hooking anywhere and no drill enhancements were used. I took several long falls, boldly forcing these sections through. The next party to attempt the route was unable to muster similar skill or commitment and chose to reach for the drill rather than retreat - even though they were only a few pitches up. These sections are uglier and far less challenging. Obviously, a choice of style is strictly personal on a first ascent. However, the creativity and boldness that goes into establishing a first ascent must be respected - or we all lose out.

Whether your ethics are traditional or new wave, the point of all this dangling and thrashing about is preservation of the challenge. On the first ascent, the climber must overcome difficulty in such a way as to leave the problem intact for the next party to struggle with and enjoy. Have enough patience and self-respect to raise your ability and psyche to meet the demands of the route rather that lower it to your capabilities through arbitrary use of force. Exercise a little restraint in the use of destructive technology. Otherwise you will create a route that lacks in creativity, boldness and inspiration.

Transcending fear and doubt in the face of the unknown is the very soul of adventure. Settling for less than your personal best will only cheapen your sense of accomplishment and the quality of the route and have the integrity to wait if your intuition says no.

It is very easy to become obsessive about a new line. You can lose track of your ideals and standards in the rush to do it before someone else does. The most difficult question to honestly answer is this: Do you desire to do the route for its own sake or because you feel recognition and a small place in history? When the going gets rough and your last good piece is way down there, it is a true test of confidence, skill and desire to spare the bolt kit. Reach within yourself for the ingenuity, trust and will power that allows us to transcend the ephemeral line between dream and reality. In the many years I have spent climbing walls, it is this power to transcend that compels me to return again to the vertical stage to chase dreams of wild adventurer where earth and sky meet.

11. ETHICS

By Steve Grossman

Not long ago, climbers were few in number and only a handful of ascents of Grade VI routes occured in the U.S. yearly. Radical advances in gear, readily available detailed route descriptions, and piton scarring have made the vertical world increasingly accesible. Popular Yosemite wall routes are now done several dozen times each season and crowding has become a significant problem. With our numbers growing, the need to minimize the impact of each and every ascent is ever more acute. The singular nature of long routes define their character, making one's experience imtimately dependent on that of the previous ascents. Trash, excrement or needless holes left by an inconsiderate party can turn a rich adventure into a sad reminder of how thoughtless our species can be.

Over the past decade a wall climbing ethic has taken shape to cope with increased usage and preserve the routes. In some respects it mirrors the wilderness ethic that evolved to safeguard the backcountry from the ill effects of increased traffic. In essence, leave the route as you found it and if possible, clean up after others that have been less considerate. Carry your trash and other waste with you rather than tossing it off with the intention of "picking it up later". The clatter of tin cans bumbing down the wall and garbage piles at the base of multi-day routes are truly disgusting to anyone trying to enjoy the natural beauty of an area. The only acceptable exception has been the use of small brown paper bags to defecate in and throw well clear of other climbers and the route itself.

On well-travelled lines duty bags are mandatory to keep the stench to a minimum. When urinating, a double bag will allow the lot to be removed from the immediate vacinity. Urinate into space and away from the route if possible or swing over to a ledge well off to one side. Never piss behind ledges or into cracks where it can't easily evaporate. Remember the Golden Rule "Dump onto others as you would have them dump onto you." Resist the temptation to jettison the haulbags after topping out or while retreating. Landings can never be predicted and the potentially lethal forces involved make it a reckless practice. In Yosemite, throwing haulsacks is prohibited and substantial fines can result. If you are too tired or overburdened with impediment to safely descend in one trip, consider returning for the excess after you've rested a bit. By fixing three ropes on the East Ledges descent, for example, one can easily reach the top of El Capitan and recover stashed gear without jeapordizing anyone's well-being.

ROCK PRESERVATION

The issue of rock preservation in a pursuit which can require the use of pitons, drills and other inherently destructive tools is necessarily a nebulous one. Repeated use of hammered protection creates permanent, ugly scars that detract from the intrinsic beauty and mystery of a wall. Weighed against such defacement is our need to experience the unknown and yet feel secure. The extent that force, skill and boldness are combined to meet a given challenge is the essence of style. It largely determines the level of adventure in an ascent. To safeguard the routes and the experience of future parties, we must consider the lasting consequences of such heavy-handed practices as overdriving pitons and copperheading. Use the hammer sparingly. Fortunately, natural protection technology has become so sophiscated and available that pitons, mashies and bolts have become less necessary. Many classic wall routes such as the Nose and Salathe Wall on El Cap and the Regular Route on Half Dome as well as numerous Grade V's can and should be done without pounding on protection. If done cleanly by all parties, these classic lines can retain their character, beauty and difficulty indefinitely despite heavy usage.

On routes that still require pitons, use nuts and camming devices as much as possible. The nutting game is every bit as demanding as tapping and can be even more satisfying. Most of the future achievements in heavily developed areas such as Yosemite lie in better style ascents of established routes. Ultimately, if a route is done cleanly, the accomplishment should be respected for its boldness and imagination. Subsequent parties will hopefully be inspired to reach within themselves for the patience and resolve necessary to avoid force and substitute ingenuity instead. The prevailing attitude that you do walls just to be able to hack away at the rock and use all that ironmongery is rather shortsighted considering that the manifest destiny of hammer and drill is a woeful prospect. The technical skill and expertise to use existing technology in good style requires considerable experience. Practice is indispensable. Spend some time experimenting with the available hardware until you develop some faith in it. Getting in over your head and bashing your way out is ignoble at best and will only lead to unnecessary pin scarring and bolting as fear erodes judgement.

Perhaps the worst case scenario is when a copperhead is placed where a nut would work and a potentially natural placement is lost when the head is cleaned and the pocket becomes too flared for anything else to work. Shallow slots can quickly degenerate to the point where leaving the placement fixed may be necessary. Copperheads have considerable holding power and like pitons don't need to be overdriven to work, especially if you're not in a serious fall situation. They can be cleaned by clipping the cable to the head of your hammer with a sling and cleaning carabiner and yanking straight out. It is also advisable to use the tip of a standard knifeblade to separate the metal from the rock on one side of the pocket prior to the outward pull. The surface of copper in contact with the rock determines the strength of the placement and unless this is reduced it will often exceed that of the cable. If the wire does break, a thin-tipped flat chisel can be used to open up the outside of the copperhead allowing the remaining cable to be extracted which makes it easier to pry the rest of the metal out. Thin piton tips tend to damage the rock less than chisels making them preferable to use for the separating step. If used artfully, copperheads can be less destructive than pitons but they should generally be regarded as a last resort. Be considerate while cleaning and remove the copperheads that you place even if the cables break. Clean any other junked heads you might come across that are inessential. You may be surprised to find a perfectly usable nut or piton placement that has been blocked because someone chose to mindlessly belt in a mashie rather than take the time to figure out something better.

The drill and chisel also occupy a curious position in the array of climbing tools. Unlike conventional gear which requires a certain adaptation to circumstance, they both allow placements to be "created" or improved" at will. This sort of technological sure-thing reduces the challenge of a given section of stone. At any point, for any reason, you can change the rules and lower the difficulty for yourself and those that follow. Don't take the easy way out by drilling a hole or chiseling a copperhead slot deeper. It is a significant visual and technical impact that is usually confined to first ascents and is discouraged heavily while doing repeats.

However, I need to stress the importance of having an emergency bolt kit along to be able to fix bad belays, bolt failures, flared hookholes and for use in rescues. There is a world of difference however, between one of these situations and placing a bolt where others have found it unnecessary simply because you might be too inexperienced or scared to work it out.

Strange as it may seem, route features are fragile. Difficult lines usually retain their initial character for only a couple of ascents before someone sees fit to add a bolt or otherwise botch up the challenge presented to them. Several lenghty ascents of difficult El Cap routes by less than experienced parties point out that given enough time spent drilling and chiseling, even very hard lines can become managable. Why waste time working up to the hardest routes when they could be conveniently slid on down to you? Amazingly enough, people once came down from walls they couldn't do in good style. Some modern day dreadnaughts seem to think nothing of using whatever means necessary to gain the hollow prestige of having repeated a route with a reputation. Unfortunately, they have neither the ability or the patience to pull it off without having totally trenched their heads.

Big wall climbing is at a pivotal point in its development. With the timid righteously clamoring for holes in the name of "safe success," we could well witness the number of unnecessary bolts climb from dozens into the hundreds as routes of daring and technical brilliance are lost in the mire of aspiring Wannabees. Or we can take pride in our heritage as climbers and continue to insist that ingenuity and skill take precedence over expedience and force so that the adventure and trial by fire that have historically made big wall climbing uniquely rich will not become lost to us. By consciously adopting a low impact ethic and boldly pushing our creative and technical limits we can sustain the challenge vital to the pursuit with a minimum of residual damage to distance us from the environment we seek to share.

APPENDIX 1: GLOSSARY

A-1: Bomber protection for aiding

A-2: Bomber protection, but awkward, with a few difficult placements.

A-3: Strings of difficult placements, backed up by the occasional bomber piece.

A-4: Many body weight placements in a row.

A-5: 60 feet of body weight placements.

A-5 Adventures: Equipment company specializing in Big Wall Gear.

Aggressive testing: Method whereby a climber applys great force to a piece of protection to test it.

Aiders: Ladders constructed out of nylon webbing.

Aiding: Placing protection and using it for upward progress.

Air Voyager: See fall-arrest.

Alumnihead: An aluminum copperhead.

Angle piton: Wedged shaped piton.

Baby angle: Small 3/8" - 1/2" angle piton.

Back clean: Removing a previously placed piece of protection.

Barnett System: Solo system utilizing prusiks on a lead line.

B.A.T. hook: A hook that can be placed on the edge of a shallowly drilled hole.

Belay seat: Piece of wood used as a seat while belaying.

Beta: Knowledge of a route.

Bird beak: Thin hook that is hammered into seams.

Bivy: The location of your bivouac.

Body Haul: Using your body as a counterweight in a haul system.

Bolts: Permanent protection drilled into the rock.

Bong: Large angle for wide cracks.

Butt bag: Cloth seat used to make belays comfy.

Camming device: A mechanical piece of protection that expands to fit the size of a crack.

Cheater stick: Long stick with a hook or carabiner on its end for reaching past placements.

Clean climbing: Climbing without use of hammer or pitons.

Cleaning biners: Carabiner on end of hammer for cleaning purposes only.

Constructive scarring: Upward blows when removing pitons in order to create a nut placement later.

Copperhead: Small usuage that is hammered into a shallow placement.

Counter weight jumar: Holds weight in haul system.

Crack 'n' up: Thin hook that hooks inside seams.

Daisy chain: Sewn or tied loops used to connect climber directly to a piece of protection.

Dowel: Rod of aluminum hammered in a shallow hole.

Down aiding, down nailing: Aiding downward in a retreat. Can be difficult.

Expando, Expanding flakes: Flakes that expand as a piton is hammered behind it.

Expedition style: Fast, light climbing style where all food and gear is carried with the climbers (as opposed to seige tactics.)

Fall-arrest: Sewn sling that reduces fall-force on piece.

Fifi hook: Open hook for quick connection to a piece of protection.

Fixed: Any piece of equipment left in place.

French Free: Resting on protection while free climbing.

Friends: See camming device.

Grade I: One to three hour duration climb.

Grade II: A half-day climb.

Grade III: A climb that lasts most of the day.

Grade IV: A climb that takes a full day to complete.

Grade V: A climb that requires more than a day to complete.

Grade VI: A multiple day climb.

Gear Sling: Sling used for carrying equipment around the body.

Gear thieves: Lowest form of life.

Hammerless: See clean climbing.

Haulbag: Bag used for carrying gear.

Haul line: Rope attached to haul bag.

Haul sheath: Covering to protect haul bag or a pack from abrasion.

HB's: Thin brass nuts developed by Hugh Banner.

Head lamp: Flash light attached to the head.

Hexcentric: Six sided nuts designed to fit a variety of sizes.

Hooks, hooking: A piece of equipment used to hook edges and flakes.

Jumar, jumaring: A device for ascending the rope; ascending the rope, (jumar is the trade name for a certain type of ascender.)

Keeper sling: Sling used to prevent loss of a piton or nut should it come out.

Knifeblade piton: Thin blade like a piton.

Lead line: Rope attached to the lead climber.

Leap frog: Back cleaning a piece of protection and placing it above your last piece.

Leeper Logan: Hook with acute curve.

Leeper Z: See Z pin

Leg haul: Pulling the haul rope with your leg.

Lost Arrow: Thin wedge-shaped piton.

Lower-out line: Rope used for lowering out haulbag on a traverse, etc.

N. B. D. : No Big Deal, easy aid climbing.

New Wave First Ascent method: Allows for the enhancement of natural features.

Nikkopress guage: Guage used for checking sizing of copperheads.

N. T. B. : Not Too Bad, moderate aid climbing.

One day ascents: Ascent completed within a 24 hour period without fixed ropes.

On-sight ascent: A climb completed without previous knowledge of the routes characteristics.

P. D. H. : Pretty Darn Hard, extreme aid climbing.

Pendulum: Swinging across a face hanging on a rope.

Pin: Piton.

Piton: Metal wedges hammered into cracks.

Porta ledge: Collapsable cot-like tent for sleeping.

Prusik: Cord or rope looped around fixed rope for ascending.

Pulley: Used to reduce friction in haul system.

Ring angle claw: A hook made from a bent over ring angle piton.

Rivet: Rod of aluminum hammered in a shallow hole.

Rivet hanger: Bolt hanger with key hole shape for rivets.

Rope bucket: A bag for stacking the rope.

Rope drag: Friction on free-running rope making it hard to pull.

RPs: Thin brass nuts.

RURPs: Realized Ultimate Reality Pitons, thin blades for seams.

Scarf: To steal.

Siege tactics: Use of fixed ropes to re-supply camps during an ascent of a big wall.

Simul-climbing: Two climbers, roped together, climbing simultaneously.

Slider, sliding nut: Two nuts that slide against each other to form a variety of sizes.

Sling: Nylon webbing used to extend the length of a piece of protection.

Soft iron piton: Soft malleable pitons that mold into cracks permanently.

Soloist, Solo aid: Solo climbing belay devices.

Space haul: Climber jumars haul line as a counter weight in a haul system.

Speedy Stitcher: Compact needle and thread in a single unit for quick repairs.

Stacked Placements: To combine nuts or pitons in a placement.

Stacked rope: A rope laid out to prevent tangling.

Stoppers: Wedge-shaped nuts.

Swage: Piece of soft metal that holds two wires together.

Swager: Press for making copperheads.

TCU: Three Cam Unit, small camming device utilizing three cams.

Tie-off, tied-off: A sling used to place less leverage on a piton that sticks out.

Topo: Map of a route.

Top stepping: Standing in highest rung of an aider.

Traditional First Ascent Method: Climber utilizes only natural features without enhancement to the rock.

Tri-cam: A cam with a point that is placed in cracks.

Wall spoon: Handy dandy all purpose item.

Z pin: Z shaped angle piton.

Zip line: Third line used for sending and retreiving gear between belayer and leader.

Appendix 2:
North American Big Walls

By no means is the following a complete list; it is merely a selection of well-known walls broken down by category. Of course, fine big-wall adventures can be had off the beaten path-discover them for yourself. The hard routes listed here really are hard; attempting these without the proper experience is not only dangerous, but invariably means that bolts will be added. Moderate routes require a fair amount of experience, and the all-clean and trade routes merely require tenacity and good judgement (those with a high degree of mechanical aptitude generally do well from the start).

For more information on gear and on getting started on walls, contact A5 Adventures, the big-wall supply shop, at 1109 S. Plaza Way #286, Flagstaff, AZ 86001 Phone: (602) 779-5084.

GETTING STARTED-SHORT PRACTICE AID ROUTES:
YOSEMITE- Direct South Face, Rixon's Pinnacle, The Stigma, Bishop's Terrace (roof), The Folly, Left Side

ZION- Organasm, Gay Haitians (Many climbing areas have practise aid climbs. Be sure that the climb has not been climbed hammerless.)

ALL CLEAN, EASIER BIG WALLS:
YOSEMITE-South Face, Washington's Column; The Prow Leaning Tower; Lost Arrow Spire; Direct, Regular Route, Half Dome, The Nose, Salathe, El Capitan.

ZION- Touchstone Wall, Equinox

SIERRA- Keeler Needle, Harding Route; Dark Star, Temple Crag; Hairline, Mt. Whitney

CASCADES- Liberty Bell, Liberty Crack

ROCKIES- Longs Peak, The Diamond

BLACK CANYON OF THE GUNNISON-The Cruise

NEW HAMPSHIRE- Labryinth Wall, Vertigo, VMC Direct, Direct Direct

TRONA BLANCO- (Baja California) Pan America

MODERATE ROUTES:
YOSEMITE- Lurking Fear, The Shield, Mescalito, Tangerine Trip, Zodiac, Never-Never-Land, Cosmos, Magic Mushroom, North American Wall, Pacific Ocean Wall, Tis-sa-ack, Liberty Cap, SW Face (Werner's Woot), South Face of Half Dome

ZION- Empty Pages, Moonstone Butress, Space Shot

LAS VEGAS-Rainbow Wall

ARIZONA-Spring Route, South Face Baboquivari Peak

TRONA BLANCO- (Baja California) The Executive Route, The Giraffe

BUGABOOS-South Face Howser Tower, Italian Pillar Becky/Chouinard, South Howser Tower Sunshine, Snowpatch Spire

HARD NAILING ROUTES:
YOSEMITE- Iron Hawk (medium-hard) Zenyatta Mendatta (medium-hard) Turning Point, Jolly Rodger, Sea of Dreams, Sheep Ranch, Space, Atlantic Ocean Wall, Born Under a Bad Sign, Native Son, The Big Chill (Half Dome)

ZION-Streaked Wall

BLACK CANYON OF THE GUNNISON-Halucinagin Walls, Painted Wall

There are numerous mixed ice and rock big wall climbs such as the Kichatna Spires, Asgaard and Mt.Thor in Baffin Island, We have declined to mention them here for these techniques have not been discussed in this book.

INDEX

systems, rating 47-48

T.C.U. 47
technique
  belay 75
  bolt 43, 54
  climbing fast 73-79
  hooking 51
  loose rock 71
  placements 65-71
    copperhead 52-53
  rock cleaning 97
  solo 82-85
testing aid 11-12, 66-67
thin piton placement 69-70
tie-offs 15, 56
Triple Unit Cam (T.C.U.) 47
tube chock 50

urinating 37, 95-96

wall living 31-39
waste management 4, 37, 95-96
water 75
  bottle 32-33
  ration 32
Westbay, Billy 73
Wilts, Chuck 42

Yarino, Tony 69